CUPCAKES
WITH A *Kick*

CUPCAKES

WITH A *Kick*

MORE THAN 50 SWEET TEMPTATIONS WITH A BOOZY TWIST

SIMONE BALMAN

Skyhorse Publishing

Kir Royale 38

Piña colada 26

Pink port 98

Painkiller 116

Mai Tai 58

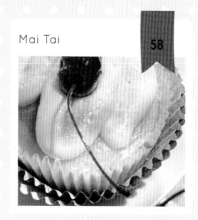

Chocolate
& amaretto 84

Super cosmo 108

Tia Maria & toffee 90

Margarita 46

Irish coffee 40

Caramel vodka 110

B-52 76

Menu

Introduction

I hate cooking, but baking is so completely different. It's more like chemistry with a bunch of not necessarily nice ingredients that somehow magically transform into something wonderful when combined! Another great combination is the things that I love: cupcakes, cocktails, and my friends from all over the world. Add this to the science of baking and you've got a serious recipe for absolute success (and fun!).

I've always been a when-the-mood-strikes-me type of baker—and it's always only been for pure enjoyment. So whether you're an experienced baker or a once-in-a-blue-moon dabbler, I hope you find the ideas in this book inspiring and as much fun to make as I do.

The ingredients are listed in the order that you need them, and the steps are simple and easy to follow. You can decorate the cupcakes in whichever way you fancy, or use the photos as a guide. Because cupcake batter is very basic, you could also experiment using your favorite cocktails as inspiration and add the necessary additional ingredients. Most of the recipes contain possible alcohol substitutions so that there is something for absolutely everyone to enjoy.

Cheers and bottoms up!

NOTE: PLEASE CONSUME RESPONSIBLY.

A bit about cupcakes

You don't have to be a baking pro to make a successful cupcake. In fact, it's quite hard for them to flop. Because cupcakes are so small, your cooking time is a lot shorter. Their small size also means that they're far less likely to flop or sink, or only rise on the one side, and the little paper cups make it so much easier to get them out of the tin.

Decorating a small cupcake is also a LOT easier than a huge cake and you don't have to commit to one icing technique, flavor or color. Cupcakes are a lot more portable than big cakes and of course they're already in a single-serving size (no cutting up that cake into 24 pieces) and they're already wrapped.

For me, the most important thing about cupcakes is that they're fun to eat. I love watching people's faces as they take that first bite into a cupcake. Because they're so small, you can have two or three different flavors rather than be stuck with a big single-flavor slice of cake. Cupcakes remind us of our childhood, of birthday parties and happy days.

Whether you're a beginner baker or someone who does it regularly, I hope you'll enjoy experimenting with these new flavors.

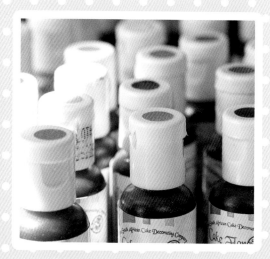

A bit about alcohol

My mother always said that if your wine isn't good enough to drink then it certainly isn't good enough to put in food, totally debunking the "cooking wine" theory. The same goes for other types of alcohol—if you like it enough to drink, then you'll like it even more in other things, surely?

Alcohol has been used in baking for hundreds of years. Beer, thanks to the high yeast content, was used originally used by the Greeks and Romans as a raising agent in bread, and beer-breads are still very popular today. Traditionally, whisky, brandy or rum was used in fruitcakes as a preservative. Curing the cake meant that it could be stored for months or even years. During Prohibition in America in the 1920s, alcohol was infused into cakes and the sweet sugars and other flavors also helped disguise the harsh flavor of the homemade alcohol.

This section is an overview of the different alcohols that can be used in baking and their effects on flavor.

Beer: These come in a wide range of flavors. They can be light or dark, bitter or quite mellow. The taste depends on the type and ratio of grains, hops and yeasts as well as how long it's fermented for. The Belgians are well known for their variety of beers—from fruit-flavored to dark and deadly.

Brandy: The word brandy comes from the Dutch word *brandewijn* which means burned (distilled) wine. Grapes (cognac, armagnac, grappa) are not the only fermented fruit used in brandy, other common fruit flavors are apples (calvados, applejack), apricots, blackberries and cherries (apricot, blackberry and cherry brandy).

Gin: This liquor derives its flavor from juniper berries and was used as far back as the Middle Ages for medicinal purposes. Dutch or Belgian gin (known as *jenever*) was one of the forerunners of this alcohol as a commercial drink. British colonists used the gin to mask the flavor of quinine, which was taken to prevent malaria. Gin is very commonly used as the base for popular drinks such as the martini.

Vodka: Classic vodka is a colorless, almost flavorless alcohol that is distilled from grains or potatoes and originated from mainly Eastern European cultures. Bartenders often use it to add extra alcohol to cocktails as it doesn't interfere with the other exotic flavors but gives the drink that extra kick. Today, we have a whole host of fashionable flavored vodkas to choose from which can be very easily incorporated into our baking.

Rum: This drink has the most colorful history and is made from the distillation of sugar-cane by-products. There are various types of rum and although they all originate in the West Indies and the New World, there are distinct regional variations based on culture and where the rums were produced. Light rums (silver or white rum) have very little flavor apart from some sweetness and are used primarily in cocktails such as daiquiris. Gold rums are medium-bodied and have been aged in charred, white-oak barrels. Dark rums, also known as brown, black or red rums, are aged longer and may have hints of spices as well as molasses or caramel tones. Spiced rums are just what the name suggests—these may be any grade of rum to which additional spices or caramel have been added.

Flavored rums are fairly new and have been infused with various flavorings and are generally consumed neat or over ice. Ovenproof rums have alcohol contents above the standard 40 percent. Premium rums are in the cognac and aged whisky category and are usually sipped neat.

Due the wide range of cocktails that are fun and exotic, we can incorporate rum very easily into our baking to mirror these flavors.

Whisky: Whisky is made from a mash of grains such as wheat, barley, oats or rye and fermented with water, malt, sugar and yeast. An exception to this is Canadian whisky, which is made from potatoes. The main whisky-producing countries are Scotland and Canada. Other countries that produce whiskey (with the e) are Ireland and the US.

This flavor doesn't take easily to being mixed with other liquors and fruit juices in cocktails and the easiest way to incorporate the taste of whisky into cupcakes would be to use a whisky-based cream liqueur.

Tequila: This is a fairly new commercial alcohol and is distilled from the blue agave (part of the cactus family) mainly in Mexico. By law Mexican tequila must contain at least 51 percent agave. There are two main types of tequila—basic, or silver tequila, and gold, which has a much deeper more complex flavor due to it being aged in wooden casks.

Tequila has become very popular as the base to cocktails such as the margarita.

Liqueurs: These are alcoholic drinks that are bottled with added sugars and flavors derived from fruits, nuts or herbs. They shouldn't be confused with liquors, such as fruit brandy, which contain no added sugar. Liqueurs can be flavored by means of distillation, infusion, percolation, or maceration to extract the flavor of the additive and then combined with alcohol. Liqueurs can range from 15 to 65 percent alcohol. The most common generic liqueurs are: almond (amaretto), anise (anisette, sambuca, ouzo and pastis), banana (crème de banane), blackcurrant (crème de cassis), cherry (kirsch and kirschwasser), coffee (Tia Maria and Kahlúa), hazelnut (Frangelico), lemon (limoncello), mint (crème de menthe), orange (Cointreau, Curaçao, triple sec and Grand Marnier), peach and bourbon (Southern Comfort), pomegranate (grenadine), and raspberry (framboise).

Wine: Wine is fermented grape juice and there are an infinite number of variations given the type of grape, the region that the grapes were grown in, soil and weather conditions and fermentation processes. Most wine drinkers have their favorite, whether it be a sparkling "champagne" or a rich, dark red. Artisanal wines that are infused with various fruits and herbs, such as pineapple or elderberry, have also become popular.

Baking with alcohol:
the myth that it evaporates

Wine, spirits, and beer are used in cooking to enhance the flavor and aroma of dishes. Contrary to what most people believe, however, all of the alcohol content doesn't always evaporate or boil away before the food is served. Chefs and cooks can't assume that when they simmer, bake, or torch (flambé to the more sophisticated cook, set-fire-to-the-kitchen to me) with alcohol that only the flavor remains.

In fact, you have to cook something for a good 3 hours to eradicate all traces of alcohol. Some cooking methods are less effective at removing alcohol than just letting it stand out uncovered overnight. As you can see from the charts below,* baking is the least effective way to remove alcohol, so always make sure your guests know that you will be serving them alcoholic cupcakes.

ALCOHOL BURN-OFF CHART

Preparation method	% of alcohol retained
Alcohol added to boiling liquid and removed from heat	85%
Alcohol flamed	75%
No heat, soaked overnight	70%
Baked, 25 minutes, alcohol not stirred into mixture	45%

BAKED/SIMMERED DISHES WITH ALCOHOL STIRRED INTO MIXTURE

15 minutes cooking time	40%
30 minutes cooking time	35%
1 hour cooking time	25%
1.5 hours cooking time	20%
2 hours cooking time	10%
2.5 hours cooking time	5%

*Alcohol retention in food preparation, by Augustin J, Augustin E, Cutrufelli RL, Hagen SR, Teitzel C., J Am Diet Assoc. 1992 Apr;92(4):486-8

Conversion charts

COMMON SOLID MEASURE EQUIVALENTS

1 cup of:	Metric weight	Imperial weight
Butter / margarine	227g	8 oz
Chocolate, baking squares	132g	4.7 oz
Cocoa powder	85g	3 oz
Coconut, desiccated	78g	2.8 oz
Flour, bread or cake	142g	5 oz
Flour, nutty wheat or whole-wheat	156g	8.5 oz
Fruit, dried	190g	7 oz
Honey / golden syrup	340g	12 oz
Nuts, chopped	140g	3 oz
Sugar, granulated	198g	7 oz
Sugar, icing (sifted)	113g	4 oz
Sugar, brown (light or dark)	198g	7 oz

DRY WEIGHT MEASUREMENTS

t = teaspoon	T = tablespoon	Ounces (oz)	Pounds (lb)	Metric (g = gram ml = milliliter)
1/16 t	a dash			
1/8 t or less	a pinch or 6 drops			0.5ml
1/4 t	15 drops			1ml
1/2 t	30 drops			2ml
1 t	1/3 T	1/6 oz		5ml
3 t	1 T	1/2 oz		14g
1 T	3 t	1/2 oz		14g
2 T	1/8 cup	1 oz		28g
4 T	1/4 cup	2 oz		56.7g
5 T + 1 t	1/3 cup	2.6 oz		75.6g
8 T	1/2 cup	4 oz	1/4 pound	113g
10 T + 2 t	2/3 cup	5.2 oz		151g
12 T	3/4 cup	6 oz	0.375 pound	170g
16 T	1 cup	8 oz	1/2 pound	225g
32 T	2 cups	16 oz	1 pound	454g
64 T	4 cups or 1 quart	32 oz	2 pounds	907g

TEMPERATURES

Fahrenheit	Celsius	Gas mark	Description
32°	0°		
212°	100°		
250°	120°	½	
275°	140°	1	Cool
300°	150°	2	
325°	160°	3	Very moderate
350°	180°	4	Moderate
375°	190°	5	
400°	200°	6	Moderately hot
425°	220°	7	Hot
450°	230°	8	
475°	240°	9	Very hot
500°	260°		

METRIC BAR/DRINK MEASUREMENTS CONVERSION TABLE

	oz = ounce	ml = milliliter
Terminology	US Standard	Metric
Dash/splash	¹⁄₃₂ oz	0.9ml
Teaspoon	⅛ oz	3.7ml
none	⅓ oz	9.17ml
Tablespoon	⅜ oz	11.1ml
Pony	1 oz	29.5ml
Jigger	1½ oz	44.5ml
Wineglass	4 oz	119ml
Split	6 oz	177ml
Cup	8 oz	257ml
Tenth	12.68 oz	375ml
Fifth	25.36 oz	750ml
Quart	33.81 oz	1 liter

SUBSTITUTIONS

1 T cornstarch (for thickening)	2 T flour
1 cup sifted all-purpose flour	1 cup plus 2 T sifted cake flour (increase quantity)
1 cup sifted cake flour	1 cup minus 2 T sifted all-purpose flour (decrease quantity)
1 T baking powder	¼ t baking soda plus ½ t Cream of Tartar
1 cup fresh milk	½ cup evaporated milk plus ½ cup water
1 cup sour milk	1 cup sweet milk into which 1 T of vinegar or lemon juice has been stirred; or 1 cup buttermilk
1 cup sour, heavy cream	⅓ cup butter and ⅔ cup milk in sour milk recipe
1 cup buttermilk	1 cup of full cream milk + 1 t vinegar and stir well
1 cup molasses	1 cup honey
28g square unsweetened chocolate	2 T cocoa plus ½ T shortening
1 cup self-raising flour	1 cup cake flour + 2 t baking powder

Before you start, please note:

1. All ingredients should **always** be at room temperature unless the recipe says otherwise. Eggs react differently when cold and the addition of other ingredients that are too warm or too cold can affect the recipe with disastrous results.

2. I've used regular-sized cupcake liners in all of the recipes to get a standard batch of 24 cupcakes (except for the sparkling pink champagne recipe, which only produces 20 cupcakes). If you use bigger or smaller liners, this will affect the number of cupcakes yielded.

3. Where the recipe calls for sugar, this means normal white granulated sugar.

4. I find that it's easier to bake using cup measures rather than using a scale, but I've included these measurements if you prefer this method. This may be confusing at first, as a cup of granulated sugar weighs more than a cup of confectioner's sugar, but please use the weights as these have been very carefully calculated.

5. Most of the cupcakes freeze very well, but always store them in an airtight container and make sure not to open this before the cupcakes are fully defrosted. Also, if you're going to freeze the cupcakes, decorate them just before serving.

6. As tempting as it may be to decorate your cupcakes straight away, do not ice the cakes until they have cooled completely.

Red wine & blackberry

My father has always been there for me—with wisdom, a waterproof shoulder and wine. He has a walk-in wine fridge stocked so well that the family joke is that he'll need to live to be two hundred to drink it all! Dad, these cupcakes are dedicated to you and hopefully we can use a special vintage (non-box) to make these together one day.

The red wine in the recipe (I used pinotage because of its full, earthy flavor) is quite subtle initially, but after the second bite the flavor comes through beautifully. These cupcakes are even better on the second day (if there are any left) as the wine flavor seems to intensify overnight. The blackberries complement the dark chocolate cake with a slightly tart twist. The blackberry juice in the icing also underlines the wine flavors. This is my all-time favorite cupcake made especially for the world's best dad!

1 cup butter

1 cup sugar

4 eggs

1 t vanilla extract

2¼ cups cake flour

½ t salt

2 t baking powder

½ cup red wine (I used a pinotage)

2 T cocoa powder

2 T red wine for soaking into cupcakes once baked

ICING

1 cup frozen blackberries defrosted in the fridge overnight

½ cup red wine (pinotage)

½ cup butter or margarine

3 cups sifted confectioner's sugar

1 T milk

DECORATIONS

24 whole blackberries (pick out the best ones from the defrosted pack)

Mother-of-pearl cake glitter dust

1. Preheat your oven to 350°F and line 24 cupcake molds or muffin tins with paper liners.

2. In your electric mixer, cream together the butter and sugar and eggs on medium until smooth and creamy. Add the vanilla and mix well again.

3. In a separate bowl sift the flour, salt and baking powder together and add to the creamed wet mixture. Add the red wine and combine but take care not to over-mix. Finally, add the cocoa powder and beat one last time.

4. Using a large spoon, carefully fill each of the cupcake liners to about ¾-full. Bake for 17–20 minutes or until a skewer inserted into the center of the cupcake comes out clean. Leave to cool slightly for about 5 minutes before turning out onto a rack.

5. When the cupcakes are completely cool, brush the 2 T of red wine on top of the cakes and allow to soak in. Set aside.

6. To make the icing, place the remaining blackberries (after selecting the best 24 for decoration) in a saucepan together with the wine and bring to a simmer. Reduce this until the blackberries are very soft and the wine is quite syrupy. Remove from the heat and sieve the mix, pressing the seeds to remove all the juice. This mix should be a little less than a ¼ cup.

7. Cream the butter well in the electric mixer and gradually add the confectioner's sugar and the milk until it has a spreading consistency. Add the blackberry sauce. This icing should be a little soft.

8. After piping the icing, decorate the top with a whole blackberry; sprinkle with food glitter.

ALTERNATIVES:
♥ More full-bodied red wines work best.

Tip: To lower the fat and calorie content in your cake, replace half of the oil with apple sauce or yogurt. This will add moisture without adding fat. Don't be tempted to substitute all of the oil with other liquids or to use a sugar substitute instead of actual sugar—this can lead to disaster.

Captain Morgan & Coke

In 2007 we moved to Bahrain and I met one of the most amazing women in my life. Gwynn is incredibly intelligent, sharp and funny and one of the best cooks I've ever come across. Her favorite drink is Bacardi and Coke but I think Captain Morgan may have been an ancestor so I've left it with that. Gwynn—you can substitute and this cupcake is dedicated to you.

The chocolate cake is beautifully dense and lush thanks to the Coke, and the ganache filling oozes rummy-richness onto your tongue. The icing also has rum in it which on the first day seems a lot stronger: day-after cupcakes have a much more subtle rum flavor. If you prefer a stronger rum flavor simply add another teaspoon or so into the ganache (it will still set perfectly) as well as into the icing.

2 cups cake flour
1 t salt
1 t baking powder
2 t baking soda
¾ cup unsweetened cocoa powder
2 cups sugar
1 cup vegetable oil
1 cup Coca-Cola
1 cup milk
2 large eggs
1 t vanilla extract

GANACHE
⅔ cup double cream
1 cup dark chocolate
2 T butter
2 T Captain Morgan Spiced Rum

ICING
½ cup butter or margarine
2½ cups sifted confectioner's sugar
1½ T Captain Morgan Spiced Rum

DECORATIONS
Rainbow sugar crystals or sparkling white sugar
Gummy cola bottles

1. Preheat your oven to 350°F and line 24 cupcake molds or muffin tins with paper liners.
2. Sift all the dry ingredients together. Add oil, Coca-Cola and milk and mix on medium speed for 2 minutes. Scrape the bottom of the mixing bowl with a spatula to make sure all ingredients are combined. Add eggs and vanilla and beat for 2 more minutes. This is a very runny mix so don't be alarmed if it looks too thin.
3. Using a large spoon, carefully fill each of the cupcake liners to about ⅔-full. Be careful not to over-fill as this cake rises quite a bit. Bake for 17–20 minutes or until a skewer inserted into the center of the cupcake comes out clean. Leave to cool slightly for about 5 minutes before turning out onto a rack.
4. Using an apple-corer, small round cookie cutter or a knife, cut holes in the top of the cooled cupcakes about 1½–2cm deep. Remove the excess cake from the divots and keep the tops as lids.
5. To make the ganache, heat the cream until just simmering and melt the chocolate into the hot cream. Stir until smooth. Add the butter and Captain Morgan. Let the ganache cool until thick but still soft enough to be piped (you can place in the fridge for about 10 minutes but watch that it

doesn't become too thick). Spoon the ganache into a plastic sandwich bag and twist the top to seal. Cut off the tip of one of the corners and pipe the ganache into the holes in the cupcakes filling them to the top. Pop the lids back on the cupcakes.
6. For the icing, cream the butter well in the electric mixer. Gradually add half of the confectioner's sugar until it is thoroughly combined. Alternate adding a little of the rum at a time with the rest of the confectioner's sugar until your icing looks thick enough to spread.
7. Ice the cupcakes, sprinkle with rainbow sugar crystals and place a gummy cola bottle in the center of the cupcake.

Note: Decorate the cupcakes just before serving as the sugar crystals will melt overnight and stain the icing, making the cupcakes look a little messy.

ALTERNATIVES:
♥ Bacardi / Jack Daniel's / Brandy

Tip: Always read recipes completely before beginning— make sure you have all the required ingredients on hand BEFORE you start and anticipate how long each step is going to take.

Chocolate-chunk Amarula

I'm always amazed how easy this recipe is: it's a "throw-it-all-together" cupcake that always impresses. The Amarula cake base is firm but not too dense and the chunks of dark chocolate provide a perfect contrast to the soft cake. A word of warning, though: it does contain rather a lot of Amarula, so this recipe falls into the naughtier category. The Amarula in the icing makes this buttercream incredibly smooth and creamy and just leaves you wanting more!

½ T sifted cake flour (for coating the chocolate)

¾ cup chopped dark chocolate (about ½ cm pieces—keep the chocolate shaving scraps for decoration)

2¾ cups cake flour

1 t baking powder

½ t salt

¾ cup mascarpone (or cream cheese)

⅔ cup butter

1 cup white sugar

1 cup light brown sugar

1 t vanilla extract

3 large eggs

¾ cup Amarula

ICING

½ cup butter or margarine

2½ cups sifted confectioner's sugar

5 T Amarula

DECORATIONS

Chocolate shavings

1. Preheat your oven to 350°F and line 24 cupcake molds or muffin tins with paper liners.
2. In a small bowl, toss the ½ T of flour in with the chocolate chunks to coat.
3. Sift the flour, baking powder and salt together and keep to one side.
4. In your mixer, or another bowl if you're using a hand mixer, combine the cream cheese and butter. Add both the sugars and the vanilla and beat until blended. Add the 3 eggs and mix again until this is well combined. With the mixer on low, add the flour mix a little at a time and alternate with the Amarula. Gently fold in the chocolate chunks until these are well distributed.
5. Using a large spoon, carefully fill each of the cupcake liners to almost full (this cake mix doesn't rise much). Bake for 17–20 minutes or until a skewer inserted into the center of the cupcake comes out clean. Leave to cool slightly for about 5 minutes before turning out onto a rack.
6. To make the icing, cream the butter with your mixer. Slowly add the confectioner's sugar a little at a time until it is well combined—it should be quite fluffy. Add the 75ml of Amarula and then continue adding the remaining confectioner's sugar slowly.
7. Ice your cupcakes and sprinkle with the leftover chocolate shavings.

ALTERNATIVES:
♥ Any cream liqueur will work for this recipe (Baileys, Cape Velvet, Strawberries & Cream or Wild Africa, to name a few).

Tip: A dash of flour will help berries, chocolate chunks or dried fruit stay suspended in the cake batter and not sink to the bottom. Toss the filling with a tablespoon of flour before folding in but remember to use flour from the recipe—don't add extra as this will cause your ingredient ratios to become uneven and result in further problems.

Piña colada

The British Virgin Islands have always been a special place for us. We spent our honeymoon there and have been lucky enough to go back a number of times—on our own, with the children as well as with various friends. My favorite pastime when we're there is comparing the various piña coladas at the restaurants along the way, so I couldn't pass up an opportunity to immortalize my favorite drink in a cupcake!

This coconut-vanilla cake is extremely light and fluffy and is a perfect light foil to the rum base. The brown sugar just gives it that extra caramel flavor that melts on the tongue. The icing is also extremely light and fluffy but the crushed pineapple pieces give this cupcake that tropical island freshness. The pieces make it impossible to pipe the icing but they're so delicious that nobody seems to care what they look like!

3 cups cake flour
1½ cups sugar
½ cup light brown sugar
2 t baking powder
½ t salt
1 cup butter
⅔ cup coconut milk
⅓ cup gold or dark rum
3 large eggs

ICING
½ cup butter or margarine
2½ cups sifted confectioner's sugar
6 T tinned crushed pineapple
2 T pineapple juice (the juice from the crushed pineapple)
¼ lemon, juiced

DECORATIONS
Desiccated coconut lightly toasted in a pan or shavings of fresh coconut
Cocktail umbrellas
Mini marshmallows (optional)

1. Preheat your oven to 350°F and line 24 cupcake molds or muffin tins with paper liners.
2. Place all the dry ingredients in your mixing bowl and mix to combine. Add the butter to your dry ingredients and mix. The mixture will be very crumbly at this stage.
3. In a separate small bowl whisk the coconut milk, rum and eggs together to combine. Pour your egg mixture slowly into the dry ingredients while mixing on medium speed at the same time. Mix for another 2 minutes until smooth.
4. Using a large spoon, carefully fill each of the cupcake liners to about ⅔-full. Be careful not to over-fill the cups as this cake rises quite a bit. Bake for 17–20 minutes or until a skewer inserted into the center of the cupcake comes out clean. Leave to cool slightly for about 5 minutes before turning out onto a rack.
5. For the icing, cream the butter with your mixer. Slowly add the confectioner's sugar a little at a time until it is thoroughly combined—it should be quite fluffy.
6. Pour the tin of crushed pineapple into a fine-mesh strainer or sieve and push through with a spoon to get as much of the juice out as possible. This is important because if your pineapple

is too wet your icing will be too runny.
7. Add 6 T of pineapple, 2 T of pineapple juice and the lemon juice to the icing mix on low speed to combine. Add the rest of the confectioner's sugar and mix on slow. Mix for another 2 minutes on medium high until smooth
8. Ice the cupcakes, pop on a few mini marshmallows, sprinkle with toasted coconut and decorate with a cocktail umbrella.

ALTERNATIVES:
♥ If you prefer an extra rum flavor, substitute the pineapple juice in the icing for rum.
♥ For a non-alcoholic version, add coconut milk instead of the rum and add 2 T of rum essence.
♥ Try a sprinkle of cinnamon sugar or nutmeg on top for extra spice flavor.

Tip: Most cake recipes can easily be converted to cupcakes. The average cake recipe should generally make enough batter for 24–36 cupcakes. Oven temperature should be kept the same, though baking time will change from anywhere between 15–30 minutes, depending on the recipe.

Sparkling pink champagne

One of my oldest friends is a real girly-girl: she loves pink and purple and I'm (fairy)godmother to her gorgeous little girl. Judy LOVES her pink champagne as much as Hannah loves her Barbie dolls! Judes, this cupcake is for you!
The champagne gives the cake a beautiful light fluffiness and the pastry cream in the center is a very indulgent surprise.

½ cup butter

1 cup sugar

2 large eggs

1 t vanilla extract

1¾ cups cake flour

½ t baking soda

¼ t baking powder

¼ t salt

½ cup sour cream

½ cup pink champagne

Pink food coloring (optional)

FILLING

2 T cornstarch

½ cup cream—divide this into 2 x
    ¼ cups

2 egg yolks

1 whole egg

½ cup pink champagne

5 T sugar

2 T butter

1 t vanilla extract

ICING

1 cup plus 1 T pink champagne

½ cup butter or margarine

2½ cups sifted confectioner's sugar

DECORATIONS

Any bling balls

Pink decorating sugar

White cake glitter

Note: This recipe yields only 20 cupcakes

1. Preheat your oven to 350°F and line 20 cupcake molds or muffin tins.
2. Cream together the butter and the sugar until light and fluffy. Add the eggs one at a time beating well after adding each egg. Add the vanilla and mix again.
3. In a separate bowl sift the flour, baking soda, baking powder and salt then mix to combine.
4. In another bowl, whisk the champagne and the sour cream. Alternate adding the flour mix and the champagne mix to butter and sugar, beginning and ending with the flour mix—the batter will be quite thick. Add a tiny dash of pink food coloring for a more pink cake (optional).
5. Using a large spoon, carefully fill each of the cupcake liners to about ¾-full. Bake for 17–20 minutes or until a skewer inserted into the center of the cupcake comes out clean. Leave to cool slightly for about 5 minutes before turning out onto a rack.
6. To make the filling, whisk the cornstarch with ¼ cup of cream and then beat in the 2 egg yolks and 1 whole egg in a medium bowl.
7. In a saucepan add the rest of the cream, champagne and sugar and bring this mixture to the boil; remove from the stove. Pour ⅓ of the boiling champagne mix into the egg mix. Keep whisking so that the eggs don't cook.

8. Pour this mixture from the bowl into the rest of the hot champagne mix in the saucepan in a thin stream whisking all the time again. Place the saucepan back on the heat and whisk constantly until the mixture reaches the consistency of very thick custard. Remove from the heat and beat in the butter and the vanilla extract. Leave to cool.
9. Using an apple-corer, small round cookie cutter or a knife, cut holes in the top of the cooled cupcakes about 1½–2cm deep. Remove the excess cake from the divots and keep the tops as lids. Spoon the cooled pastry cream into the holes in the cupcakes and pop the little lids back on.
10. To make the icing, reduce the champagne in a saucepan on a medium to high heat to about 2 T. Allow to cool. Cream the butter and the confectioner's sugar. Pour the champagne reduction into the icing and add 1 T of bubbly champagne from the bottle and mix well. Decorate the cupcakes with icing and the cake pearls or silver balls and sprinkle with a little pink colored sugar and cake glitter.

Note: This recipe uses almost a whole bottle of champagne but is perfect for special occasions!

Chocolate & Van der Hum

Cape Town holds many memories for me and it finally feels like home again after being overseas for so long. This cupcake is dedicated to our friend Theo, a Dutch descendant who is passionate about making a difference in the community. It was his suggestion that I try this combination so Theo, this cupcake is a tribute to you.

Van der Hum is the South African equivalent of orange curaçao (most commonly sold under the brand name Cointreau). It was first invented by the Dutch and is a white rum-based liqueur flavored with the peel of white, bitter oranges. Van der Hum is made with a local brandy and naartjies, which are the South African version of tangerines. For those of you who love the combination of chocolate and orange, this cupcake is the ultimate indulgence.

2 cups cake flour
1 t salt
1 t baking powder
2 t baking soda
¾ cup unsweetened cocoa powder
2 cups sugar
1 cup vegetable oil
1 cup hot coffee
1 cup milk
2 large eggs
1 t orange essence

GANACHE
⅔ cup double cream
1 cup dark chocolate
2 T butter
2 T Van der Hum

ICING
½ cup butter or margarine
2½ cups sifted confectioner's sugar
4 T Van der Hum
3 T unsweetened cocoa powder

DECORATIONS
Candied citrus peel
Shaved dark chocolate

1. Preheat your oven to 350°F and line 24 cupcake molds or muffin tins with paper liners.
2. Sift all the dry ingredients together. Add oil, coffee and milk and mix on medium speed for 2 minutes. Scrape the bottom of the mixing bowl with a spatula to make sure all ingredients are combined. Add eggs and orange essence and beat for 2 more minutes.
3. Using a large spoon, carefully fill each of the cupcake liners to about ⅔-full. Be careful not to over-fill the cups as this cake rises quite a bit. Bake for 17–20 minutes or until a skewer inserted into the center of the cupcake comes out clean. Leave to cool slightly for about 5 minutes before turning out onto a rack.
4. Using an apple-corer, small round cookie cutter or a knife, cut holes in the top of the cooled cupcakes about 1½–2cm deep. Remove the excess cake from the divots and keep the tops as lids.
5. To make the ganache, heat the cream until just simmering and melt the chocolate into the hot cream. Stir until smooth. Add the butter and Van der Hum. Let the ganache cool until thick but still soft enough to be piped (you can place in the fridge for about 10 minutes but watch that it doesn't become too thick).
6. Place 4–6 pieces of candied citrus peel in each cupcake hole. Spoon the ganache into a plastic sandwich bag and twist the top to seal. Cut off the tip of one of the corners and pipe the ganache into the holes in the cupcakes filling them to the top. Pop the lids back on the cupcakes.
7. To make the icing, cream the butter well in the electric mixer. Gradually add half of the confectioner's sugar until it is thoroughly combined. Alternate adding a little of the Van der Hum at a time with the rest of the confectioner's sugar and the cocoa powder until your icing looks thick enough to spread or pipe.
8. Ice your cupcakes and sprinkle with candied citrus peel and chocolate shavings.

ALTERNATIVES:
♥ Cointreau
♥ Mandarine Napoleon

Tip: It is easier to cut holes with lids one at a time as you fill the cupcakes with the pastry cream or ganache so that the lids fit back on exactly and there are no gaps in the top of the cupcake.

Brandy & banana

Sometimes you just don't need a reason to like something and this recipe appealed to me straight away. I found a version of it on the internet (I can't remember where so I'm sorry to whoever originally put this together) and have adapted it to South African tastes. The original recipe called for bourbon but as this isn't widely drunk in South Africa, I preferred to use the warm mellow flavor of brandy. I love the flavors in this beautifully moist and light cupcake and the brandy in the toppings just rounds it out beautifully.

Given the amount of bananas in the batter, I'd like to think of this a very "healthy" treat and so have also made a "low-fat" ganache (which only means that I left out the butter). The slightly sour banana chips on top give a nice tart contrast to the fluffy sweetness of the icing.

2⅔ cups cake flour

2½ t baking soda

½ t salt

1 t cinnamon

¼ t ground allspice

2 large eggs

1½ cups brown sugar

2 t vanilla extract

½ cup sour cream

1 cup butter, melted

3 large ripe bananas, mashed
(about 1½ cups)

⅔ cup milk

¼ cup brandy

ICING

½ cup butter or margarine

2½ cups sifted confectioner's sugar

3 t brandy

GANACHE

225g dark chocolate

⅔ cup double cream

1 t brandy

DECORATIONS

Lemon banana chips

1. Preheat your oven to 350°F and line 24 cupcake molds or muffin tins with paper liners.

2. Sift together the flour, baking soda, salt, cinnamon and ground allspice; set aside.

3. In a large bowl, cream the eggs and the brown sugar until smooth, add the vanilla extract, sour cream and melted butter and mix. Add the dry ingredients to the egg mix and beat on low until all the dry ingredients are combined. Add the mashed banana and the milk and beat until these are also mixed in well.

4. Using a large spoon, carefully fill each of the cupcake liners to about ¾-full. Bake for 17–20 minutes or until a skewer inserted into the center of the cupcake comes out clean. Leave to cool for about 5 minutes before turning out onto a rack.

5. While the cakes are still warm, prick holes in the tops and then using a pastry brush, soak the tops of the cakes with brandy.

6. To make the icing, cream the butter well. Gradually add half of the confectioner's sugar until it is thoroughly combined. Alternate adding a little of the brandy at a time with the rest of the confectioner's sugar until your icing looks thick enough to spread or pipe.

7. For the ganache, heat the cream until just simmering and melt the

chocolate into the hot cream. Stir until smooth, and add the brandy. Let the ganache cool until thick but still soft enough to be piped (you can place in the fridge for about 10 minutes but watch that it doesn't become too thick).

8. Spoon the ganache into a plastic sandwich bag and twist the top to seal. Cut off the tip of one of the corners and drizzle the ganache over the top of the iced cupcakes.

9. Slice a fresh banana quite thinly and dip in lemon juice. Place these on a baking tray and dust with a little confectioner's sugar. Place these in a low oven for about half an hour, turning after 15 minutes. Push a banana chip into the top of each cupcake.

ALTERNATIVES:
♥ Banana liqueur
♥ Add chocolate chunks to the batter by tossing a ½ T of flour with ½ cup of chocolate chunks to coat. Gently stir the chocolate chunks into the batter with a spoon until well distributed.
♥ You can also use chopped toffee (e.g. Werthers) in the batter, or sprinkled on top.

Apple sours

This very sour concoction reminds me of days we used to party in Durban. We'd get home in the early hours of the morning, still be able to get to work by 8 and then at the end of the day get ready for another evening of partying all over again. I'm not sure how we managed, but they were very good times and I think I might still be recovering!

I love the sour apple surprise in the middle of this beautifully moist cupcake—the icing isn't too sweet and the sour sugar on top really boosts that sour tang (which is exactly the drink this recipe was based on and was the inspiration for this gorgeous treat). These cupcakes are extremely easy and quick to make—and disappear just as fast!

1 tin unsweetened pie apples
½ cup Tang Apple Sour
3 cups cake flour
1½ cups sugar
4 t baking powder
1 t salt
½ cup Tang Apple Sour
½ cup milk
1 cup vegetable oil
4 large eggs
2 t vanilla extract

ICING

½ cup butter or margarine
2½ cups sifted confectioner's sugar
5 T Tang Apple Sour

TOPPING

Electric Green gel food coloring
¼ cup sugar
1 t citric acid (add less if you don't want it quite so sour)

1. Place the entire tin of unsweetened pie apples in a saucepan and add ½ cup of Tang or any other apple sours. Poach the apples on medium to low heat for about 10 minutes being careful not to boil (steam should just start rising from the pot). Remove from heat and allow to cool in the saucepan (this allows the apples to soak up the sour apple flavor). Drain the apples in a sieve then cut the apple pieces to about 2cm chunks.

2. Preheat your oven to 350°F and line 24 cupcake molds or muffin tins with paper liners.

3. Sift all the dry ingredients together straight into the mixing bowl. Add Tang Apple Sour, milk, oil, eggs and vanilla to the dry ingredients and beat well until smooth and creamy.

4. Using a large spoon, fill the cupcake liners to halfway and then place the apple pieces in the centers of your cake batter. Gently spoon more cake batter over the top with a teaspoon so that the apple is completely covered. Bake for 17–20 minutes or until a skewer inserted into the center of the cupcake comes out clean. Leave to cool slightly for about 5 minutes before turning out onto a rack.

5. To make the icing, cream the butter well in the electric mixer. Gradually add half of the confectioner's sugar until it is thoroughly combined. Alternate adding a little of the apple sours at a time with the rest of the sugar until your icing looks thick enough to spread or pipe.

6. To make the sour sugar topping, mix a little drop of Electric Green gel food coloring with granulated sugar and leave to dry on a baking sheet. (Wear gloves to mix in the food coloring if you don't want green hands). Mix in the citric acid to taste.

7. Ice your cupcakes and spoon the sour sugar over. Shake off any excess.

Note: These cupcakes are best served fresh and don't freeze very well—the apples tend to make the cake go soggy when defrosting them.

ALTERNATIVES:
♥ Any sour spirit cooler
♥ You can keep the apples in the cake as the fruit base for any other flavor as they absorb the flavor of whichever sour spirit cooler you choose.

Tip: If you want to make strawberry sours cupcakes (with a sour strawberry cooler), use fresh and not frozen or tinned strawberries as these are too soggy.

Drunken butter rum

A few years ago we spent the most amazing holiday in Barbados and the British Virgin Islands with our very good friends David and Sonja. We did a tour of the Mount Gay Rum Distillery in Barbados as David was a rum-nut and we even bought him a book of the pubs in the Virgin Islands, which we always hoped to crawl with him one day. Unfortunately, David passed away in 2011, so this special cupcake is dedicated to him.

There is quite a lot of rum in this cupcake but combined with the pecan nuts and toasted coconut, it doesn't have that sharp, alcoholic bite. The rum is just another mellow accent to the firm but moist cake.

1 cup pecan nuts, chopped
½ cup coconut flakes
¾ cup butter
1½ cups sugar
3 large eggs
1½ t vanilla extract
2⅔ cups sifted cake flour
1 t baking soda
½ t baking powder
½ t salt
1 cup sour cream
¾ cup rum (I prefer Captain Morgan Spiced Gold—the spices add to the flavor of the pecans)

GLAZE
½ cup butter or margarine
1 cup sifted confectioner's sugar
2 x ¼ cups rum

ICING
½ cup butter or margarine
2½ cups sifted confectioner's sugar
4 T rum
1½ T vanilla extract

DECORATIONS
¼ cup toasted pecan nuts and coconut mixed

1. Preheat your oven to 350°F and line 24 cupcake molds or muffin tins with paper liners.
2. In a dry pan toast the chopped pecan nuts and coconut flakes, set aside to cool. Keep about ¼ cup of this mix aside for sprinkling on top as decoration.
3. Cream together the butter and sugar until light and fluffy. Add the 3 eggs one at a time beating well after adding each egg. Add the vanilla and mix again.
4. In a separate bowl sift the flour, baking soda (baking soda), baking powder and salt together and then mix gently with a spoon until well combined.
5. In another medium-sized bowl, whisk the rum and sour cream together. Alternate adding the flour mix and the rum/cream mix to the butter and sugar, beginning and ending with the flour mix—the batter will be quite thick. Fold the pecan—coconut mix into the batter until well distributed. Using a large spoon, carefully fill each of the cupcake liners to about ¾–full. Bake for 17-20 minutes or until a skewer inserted into the center of the cupcake comes out clean. Leave to cool slightly for about 5 minutes before turning out onto a rack.
6. For the glaze, melt the butter in a small saucepan and then mix in the sifted confectioner's sugar and a ¼ cup of rum. Bring to the boil, stirring constantly for about 5 minutes until the glaze thickens. Remove from heat, stir in the remaining ¼ cup of rum and set aside to cool and thicken further.
7. Dip the cupcakes into the glaze and allow the excess to drip off before turning upright again (this step can get a bit messy). Set cupcakes to one side and allow to cool completely. Keep the remaining glaze to drizzle on top of the icing.
8. To make the icing, cream the butter well in the electric mixer. Gradually add half of the confectioner's sugar until it is well combined. Alternate adding a little of the rum and vanilla at a time with the rest of the confectioner's sugar until your icing looks thick enough to spread or pipe.
9. Sprinkle with toasted pecan nuts and coconut and drizzle a little of the leftover glaze over the top.

ALTERNATIVES:
♥ Brandy
♥ Bourbon
♥ Whiskey

Tip: If you can't find large coconut flakes, desiccated coconut will do.

Kir Royale

These cupcakes are for the girls of "Rent-a-Crowd"—all bright, fruity and slightly tart with soft, sweet centers. Our families are now spread out far and wide and I miss you.

Traditionally, a Kir Royale is made with crème de cassis or blackcurrant liqueur and champagne. You can go traditional in this recipe or substitute the blackcurrant liqueur with cherry liqueur or any sharp, tangy fruit liqueur you prefer. We do the cherry option and in our house it's become known as Barbie-juice—not because of the "babelas" (hangover) that it could potentially lead to but after the doll, because it's such a girly drink.

3 cups cake flour

1½ cups sugar

4 t baking powder

1 t salt

½ cup milk

1 cup vegetable oil

4 large eggs

2 t vanilla extract

CREAM FILLING

½ cup cream—divide this into 2 x ¼ cups

½ cup champagne or sparkling wine

½ cup cherry liqueur

5 T sugar

2 T cornstarch

1 whole egg

2 egg yolks

2 T butter

1 t vanilla extract

ICING

1 cup champagne or sparkling wine

⅔ cup cherry liqueur

½ cup butter or margarine

2½ cups sifted confectioner's sugar

DECORATIONS

Champagne-cherry reduction

White cake glitter

Maraschino cherries (optional)

1. Preheat your oven to 350°F and line 24 cupcake molds or muffin tins with paper liners.

2. Sift all the dry ingredients together. Add the milk, champagne, oil, eggs and vanilla and beat well until smooth and creamy. Add a tiny dash of pink food coloring for a more pink cake—this is optional.

3. Using a large spoon, fill each of the cupcake liners to about ¾-full. Bake for 17–20 minutes or until a skewer inserted into the center of the cupcake comes out clean. Leave to cool slightly for about 5 minutes before turning out onto a rack.

4. In a saucepan add the cream, champagne, cherry liqueur and sugar and bring this mixture to the boil and then remove from the stove.

5. In a medium bowl, whisk the cornstarch with the other ¼ cup of cream and then beat in the 2 egg yolks and 1 whole egg. Pour ⅓ of the boiling champagne mix into the egg mix but remember to keep whisking as you add this so that the eggs don't cook.

6. Pour the mixture from the bowl into the hot champagne mix in the saucepan in a thin stream whisking all the time again. Place the saucepan back on the heat and whisk constantly until the mixture reaches

the consistency of very thick custard, remove from the heat and beat in the butter and the vanilla extract. Leave to one side to cool.

7. Using an apple-corer, small round cookie cutter or a knife, cut holes in the top of the cooled cupcakes about 1½–2cm deep. Remove the excess cake from the divots and keep the tops as lids. Spoon the cream filling into the holes in the cupcakes filling them almost to the top and pop the little lids back on.

8. To make the icing, put the cup of champagne and cherry liqueur in a saucepan and on a medium to high heat and reduce this down to about 4 T and allow to cool. Cream the butter and the confectioner's sugar. Pour 2 T of champagne-cherry reduction into the icing and add 1 T of bubbly champagne from the bottle (if you have any left) and mix well.

9. Drizzle the last 2 T of the reduction over the cakes and pipe. Sprinkle with some cake glitter.

Irish coffee

When we go out to dinner we usually end the evening with an Irish Coffee. I can't think of a restaurant now that doesn't offer these on their menu and they've become a firm South African favorite. Even when we lived in Belgium, we'd make them for a taste of home.

This chocolate cake has a strong, rich coffee flavor and the light, fluffy cream also has a touch of Irish whiskey that adds to the taste. The chocolate coffee ganache filling is rich and deep, and the coffee and whiskey come through beautifully. You can leave the ganache out for a lighter taste but I just love the excitement of biting into a gooey surprise.

2 cups cake flour
1 t salt
1 t baking powder
2 t baking soda
¾ cup unsweetened cocoa powder
2 cups sugar
1 cup vegetable oil
1 cup strong, hot coffee
1 cup milk
2 large eggs
1 t vanilla extract

GANACHE
⅔ cup double cream
1 cup dark chocolate
2 T butter
2 T whiskey

ICING
½ cup butter or margarine
2½ cups sifted confectioner's sugar
4 T whiskey

DECORATIONS
2 T unsweetened cocoa powder
Stencil (I cut out a heart)

1. Preheat your oven to 350°F and line 24 cupcake molds or muffin tins with paper liners.
2. Sift all the dry ingredients together. Add oil, coffee and milk and mix on medium speed for 2 minutes. Scrape the bottom of the mixing bowl with a spatula to make sure all ingredients are combined. Add eggs and vanilla extract and beat for 2 more minutes.
3. Using a large spoon, carefully fill each of the cupcake liners to about ⅔-full. Be careful not to over-fill the cups as this cake rises quite a bit. Bake for 17–20 minutes or until a skewer inserted into the center of the cupcake comes out clean. Leave to cool slightly for about 5 minutes before turning out onto a rack.
4. Using an apple-corer, small round cookie cutter or a knife, cut holes in the top of the cooled cupcakes about 1½–2cm deep. Remove the excess cake from the divots and keep the tops as lids.
5. To make the ganache, heat the cream until just simmering and melt the chocolate into the hot cream. Stir until smooth and then add the butter and whiskey. Let the ganache cool until thick but still soft enough to be piped (you can place in the fridge for about 10 minutes but watch that it doesn't become too thick). Spoon the ganache into a plastic sandwich bag and twist the top to seal. Cut off the tip of one of the corners and pipe the ganache into the holes in the cupcakes, filling them to the top. Pop the lids back on the cupcakes.
6. For the icing, cream the butter well in the electric mixer. Gradually add half of the confectioner's sugar until it is thoroughly combined. Alternate adding a little of the whiskey at a time with the rest of the confectioner's sugar until your icing looks thick enough to spread or pipe. Holding the stencil over the top of the icing, sieve the cocoa powder onto the template.

ALTERNATIVES:
♥ Baileys Coffee or Sultan Special Coffee, with Baileys Irish Cream
♥ French Coffee, with Grand Marnier
♥ Italian Classico, with amaretto

Kahlúa, chocolate & peanut butter

My husband is a sailing fanatic and a year ago, he bought a L26 yacht. In his search for a crew we met De Wet, who has become our third child. When he comes past the house every day, he heads straight to the kettle to make himself a coffee and often clears out whatever I have in the fridge (as boys do). This cupcake was invented especially for my "adopted" son who has become one of my chief tasters.

The chocolate cake has quite a strong, rich coffee flavor and the ganache filling, although it sounds very sweet and rich, is surprisingly moreish. The icing is also very light with just a subtle peanut-coffee flavor. I recommend the chopped salted peanuts to sprinkle on top as the little dash of salt offsets the sweetness of the icing beautifully.

2 cups cake flour

1 t salt

1 t baking powder

2 t baking soda

¾ cup unsweetened cocoa powder

2 cups sugar

1 cup vegetable oil

1 cup strong, hot coffee

1 cup milk

2 large eggs

1 t vanilla extract

GANACHE

⅔ cup double cream

1 cup white chocolate

2 T smooth peanut butter

2 T Kahlúa

ICING

½ cup butter or margarine

2½ cups sifted confectioner's sugar

4 T Kahlúa

1 T smooth peanut butter

DECORATIONS

Chopped salted nuts

Dark chocolate shavings

1 small bag of chocolate covered nuts

1. Preheat your oven to 350°F and line 24 cupcake molds or muffin tins with paper liners.

1. Sift all the dry ingredients together. Add oil, coffee and milk and mix on medium speed for 2 minutes. Scrape the bottom of the mixing bowl with a spatula to make sure all ingredients are combined. Add eggs and vanilla extract and beat for 2 more minutes.

2. Using a large spoon, carefully fill each of the cupcake liners to about ⅔-full. Be careful not to over-fill the cups as this cake rises quite a bit. Bake for 17–20 minutes or until a skewer inserted into the center of the cupcake comes out clean. Leave to cool slightly for about 5 minutes before turning out onto a rack.

3. Using an apple-corer, small round cookie cutter or a knife, cut holes in the top of the cooled cupcakes about 1½–2cm deep. Remove the excess cake from the divots and keep the tops as lids.

4. Heat the cream until just simmering and melt the chocolate into the hot cream. Stir until smooth and then add the peanut butter and Kahlúa. Let the ganache cool until thick but still soft enough to be piped (you can place in the fridge for about 10 minutes but watch that it doesn't become too thick). Spoon the ganache into a plastic sandwich bag and twist the top to seal. Cut off the tip of one of the corners and pipe the ganache into the holes in the cupcakes, filling them to the top. Pop the lids back on the cupcakes.

5. Cream the butter well in the electric mixer. Gradually add half of the confectioner's sugar until it is thoroughly combined. Alternate adding a little of the Kahlúa at a time with the rest of the confectioner's sugar and the peanut butter until your icing looks thick enough to spread or pipe. Ice your cupcakes and decorate.

ALTERNATIVES:
♥ Any coffee liqueur
♥ Chunky peanut butter in the ganache adds an extra nutty crunch

Tip: To bring cold eggs to room temperature quickly, you can put the whole eggs into a bowl of lukewarm water (not hot) for 30 minutes.

White Russian

I was first introduced to this deadly shooter when I was studying and working in the States, so this concoction always brings back memories for me. When I tell people that it contains both Kahlúa AND vodka, the reaction is that this may be a case of overkill but, believe me, it works!

These cupcakes are smooth and creamy and they're now everyone's new favorite!

¾ cup butter at room temperature

1½ cups sugar

3 large eggs (at room temperature)

1½ t vanilla extract

2⅔ cups sifted cake flour

1 t baking soda

½ t baking powder

½ t salt

¾ cup Kahlúa and vodka mixed half-and-half

1 cup sour cream

¼ cup Kahlúa and vodka mixed half-and-half for soaking into the cupcakes once baked

ICING

½ cup butter or margarine

2½ cups sifted confectioner's sugar

3 T Kahlúa

3 T vodka

DECORATIONS

Grated white chocolate or white chocolate curls

1. Preheat your oven to 350°F and line 24 cupcake molds or muffin tins with paper liners. Cream together the butter and sugar until light and fluffy. Add the 3 eggs one at a time beating well after adding each egg. Add the vanilla and mix again.

2. In a separate bowl sift the flour, baking soda (baking soda), baking powder and salt together and then mix gently with a spoon to make sure all these dry ingredients are well combined.

3. In another medium-sized bowl, whisk together the ¾ cup Kahlúa and vodka mix with the sour cream. Alternate adding the flour mix and the rum/cream mix to the butter and sugar, beginning and ending with the flour mix—the batter will be quite thick. Using a large spoon, carefully fill each of the cupcake liners to about ¾ – full. Bake for 17–20 minutes or until a skewer inserted into the center of the cupcake comes out clean. Leave to cool slightly for about 5 minutes before turning out onto a rack.

4. Cream the butter well in the electric mixer. Gradually add half of the confectioner's sugar until it is thoroughly combined. Alternate adding a little of the Kahlúa and vodka at a time with the rest of the confectioner's sugar until your icing looks thick enough to spread or pipe. Ice your cupcakes and decorate with grated white chocolate curls.

ALTERNATIVES:
♥ Tia Maria
♥ Mokador

Tip: To retrieve stray eggshells in a mixture, use the emptied half-shell (eggshell sticks to eggshell).

Margarita

I spent about nine months in the United States after college and our favorite Monday night pastime was going to our local bar and watching Monday night football, drinking margaritas and snacking on all-you-can-eat buffalo wings. Needless to say I gained quite a lot of weight over this period, but it was a lot of fun and these cupcakes always remind me of this time in my life.

This cake's texture has been described as "beyond perfect." The lime and tequila really shine through and these are not as sweet as a normal cupcake.

3 cups cake flour

1 T baking powder

½ t salt

1 cup butter

2 cups sugar

4 large eggs

Zest and juice of 3 limes (can use 1 lemon if limes aren't available)

½ t vanilla extract

3 T tequila

1 cup sour cream or buttermilk

4 T tequila for soaking into cupcakes once baked

ICING

½ cup butter or margarine

2½ cups sifted confectioner's sugar

1 T lime juice

4 T tequila

DECORATIONS

Lime zest or a sliver of fresh lime

Coarse salt or white decorating sugar (depends on your preference but the salt adds an extra taste element)

1. Preheat your oven to 350°F and line 24 cupcake molds or muffin tins with paper liners.

2. Sift the flour, baking powder and salt together and then mix together gently with a spoon to make sure all these dry ingredients are well combined.

3. In your electric mixer, cream together the butter and sugar on medium-high until light and fluffy (about 5 minutes). Add the eggs one at a time beating well after adding each egg. Add the lime zest, the lime juice, the vanilla extract and tequila and mix again. Reduce the mixer speed to low and alternate adding the flour mix and the sour cream/buttermilk to the butter and sugar, beginning and ending with the flour mix—the batter will be quite thick. Using a large spoon, carefully fill each of the cupcake liners to about ¾ - full. Bake for 17–20 minutes or until a skewer inserted into the center of the cupcake comes out clean. Leave to cool slightly for about 5 minutes before turning out onto a rack.

4. Before the cupcakes cool completely (about 5-10 minutes after removing from the oven), poke holes into the tops of the cakes and using a pastry brush soak the tequila that was kept to one side into the holes (I usually do about 2 dips per cupcake).

5. Cream the butter well in the electric mixer. Gradually add half of the confectioner's sugar until it is thoroughly combined. Alternate adding a little of the tequila and lime juice 1 T at a time with the rest of the confectioner's sugar until your icing looks thick enough to spread or pipe.

6. Ice the cupcakes, sprinkle the lime zest on top or decorate with a thin sliver of fresh lime and some course sea salt or sugar if you prefer a sweeter taste.

ALTERNATIVES:

♥ Fresh strawberries chopped up really finely into the cake and icing also make a great strawberry margarita.

♥ To make a non-alcoholic version, simply leave out the tequila. This can be done without affecting the texture of the cake. Exchange all the tequila in the icing for lemon juice.

Tip: You can substitute milk with yogurt or sour cream, to experiment with different textures. When substituting liquids in a recipe, always make sure that the total liquid content and type of liquid remains the same as the original recipe. For example, 1 cup of milk in the batter is substituted with ½ a cup of milk and ½ cup of juice.

Peach bellini

One of the best New Year's parties I've ever had was in 2007/8 on our compound in Bahrain. We had a mini United Nations and we all decided to celebrate New Year's in the order in which everyone's home country came into the New Year. Our friends Marko and Lily, the Aussies, were second to the Kiwis and they served prawns on the barbie and peach bellinis. These cupcakes make me think of that amazing evening and especially Lily and Marko.

In keeping with making the recipes a bit more South African, I've used dried peaches. The champagne is a perfect vehicle for the delicate flavor of the peaches.

3 cups cake flour
1 T baking powder
½ t salt
1 cup butter
2 cups sugar
1 t vanilla extract
6 egg whites
¾ cup champagne or sparkling wine
¼ cup peach schnapps
12 dried peaches, finely chopped
4 T peach schnapps for soaking into cupcakes once baked

ICING
½ cup butter or margarine
2½ cups sifted confectioner's sugar
1 T champagne or sparkling wine
4 T peach schnapps

DECORATIONS
Candied dried peaches
White sugar crystals

1. Preheat your oven to 350°F and line 24 cupcake molds or muffin tins with paper liners.
2. Sift the flour, baking powder and salt together and then mix together gently with a spoon to make sure all these dry ingredients are well combined.
3. With your electric mixer, cream together the butter and sugar on medium-high until light and fluffy (about 3–5 minutes). Add the egg whites one at a time beating well after each addition and scraping the sides of the bowl. Add the vanilla extract and mix again.
4. In a measuring cup combine the champagne and peach schnapps.
5. Reduce the mixer speed to low and alternate adding the flour mix and the champagne/schnapps to the butter and sugar, beginning and ending with the flour mix—the batter will be quite thick. Fold in the chopped dried peaches. Using a large spoon, carefully fill each of the cupcake liners to about ¾-full. Bake for 17–20 minutes or until a skewer inserted into the center of the cupcake comes out clean. Leave to cool slightly for about 5 minutes before turning out onto a rack.
6. Before the cupcakes cool completely (about 5–10 minutes after removing from the oven), poke holes into the tops

of the cakes and using a pastry brush soak the tequila that was kept to one side into the holes (usually do about 2 dips per cupcake).
7. For the icing, cream the butter well in the electric mixer. Gradually add half of the confectioner's sugar until it is thoroughly combined. Alternate adding a little of the peach schnapps and champagne 1 T at a time with the rest of the confectioner's sugar until your icing looks thick enough to spread or pipe.
8. Ice the cupcakes, decorate the top with a sliver of candied dried peach and sprinkle with white sparkle sugar or food glitter.

ALTERNATIVES:
♥ Any fruit schnapps and complementary dried fruit
♥ For a non-alcoholic cupcake, use peach juice instead of the schnapps and sparkling wine/champagne.

Tip: You can bake the cupcakes in advance as they freeze well (un-iced) in an airtight container. When you need them, take them out the day before and allow them to defrost slowly overnight but do NOT open the container until they are fully defrosted. Ice them just before eating.

Citrus with chardonnay jelly

Recently we were invited to a braai and these delicious refreshing cupcakes made it a perfect afternoon. My friends and I are not big chardonnay fans—it's a little too woody for us and as I had a spare bottle gathering dust here at home (something that doesn't happen very often), this seemed a great opportunity to experiment. These cupcakes were a huge hit and we now know exactly what to do with our spare chardonnay!

Agar-agar is a LOT of fun to play with—it's a vegan version of gelatine that sets at room temperature and is available from most health shops. In fact when I told my local shop owner what I intended doing with it he actually asked if I would bring a batch in for him to sell in the shop! Obviously these fall into the "mental-health and well-being" category.

3 cups cake flour

1½ cups sugar

4 t baking powder

1 t salt

¾ cup milk

2 T lemon juice

2 T freshly squeezed orange juice

1 cup vegetable oil

4 large eggs

2 T vanilla extract

Zest of 1 lemon and 1 orange
(reserve some for decorating)

JELLY FILLING

2 t agar-agar powder

2 cups chardonnay

ICING

½ cup butter or margarine

2½ cups sifted confectioner's sugar

4 T chardonnay

DECORATIONS

Lemon and orange zest

White cake glitter dust

1. Preheat your oven to 350°F and line 24 cupcake molds or muffin tins with paper liners.

2. Sift all the dry ingredients together straight into the mixing bowl. Add the milk, lemon and orange juice, oil, eggs and vanilla to the dry ingredients and beat well until smooth and creamy. Fold in the lemon and orange zest. Using a large spoon, carefully fill each of the cupcake liners to about ¾–full. Bake for 17–20 minutes or until a skewer inserted into the center of the cupcake comes out clean. Leave to cool slightly for about 5 minutes before turning out onto a rack.

3. Using an apple-corer, small round cookie cutter or a knife, cut holes in the top of the cooled cupcakes about 1½–2cm deep. Remove the excess cake from the divots and keep the tops as lids. Place the cupcakes in the refrigerator to chill.

4. Mix the agar-agar powder with the chardonnay in a saucepan and bring to the boil, making sure that all the agar powder is dissolved. Leave to one side to cool slightly. (Don't allow the agar jelly to cool completely as it sets at room temperature). Pour the jelly into the chilled cupcakes and pop the lids back on top. Allow to set.

5. Cream the butter well in the electric mixer. Gradually add half of the confectioner's sugar until it is thoroughly combined. Alternate adding a little of the chardonnay at a time with the rest of the confectioner's sugar until your icing looks thick enough to spread or pipe.

6. Ice the cupcakes, sprinkle the reserved citrus zest on top of the icing and dust with a little white cake glitter.

ALTERNATIVES:
♥ Any white wine
♥ Make a non-alcoholic version by using orange juice to make the jelly.

Tip: Don't use spreads to replace butter, margarine or shortening in a recipe. Spreads contain less fat and more water, so they won't perform like butter or margarine.

Gin & tonic

This recipe uses a LOT of gin! The last time we used so much gin at one time was when we were on our sailing vacation with David and Sonja. Sonja was the bar wench and her G&Ts were just that—gin and just a little tonic for flavor! The guys agreed that they were the best gins they'd ever had, but sailing straight for the rest of the afternoon proved a little tricky. This recipe is dedicated to Sonja and is a reminder not to nominate her as barmaid ever again!

These cupcakes are very addictive with the tartness of the lemon and the bitterness of the tonic offsetting the sweetness beautifully. Even though there is a lot of gin in the recipe, it actually comes through quite subtly, but it's definitely there!

3 cups cake flour

1½ cups sugar

4 t baking powder

1 t salt

½ cup milk

½ cup gin

1 cup vegetable oil

4 large eggs

Juice from 1 lemon

GLAZE

2½ cups sifted confectioner's sugar

4 T gin

2 T lemon juice

ICING

½ cup butter or margarine

4 cups sifted confectioner's sugar

3 T gin

2 T tonic

DECORATIONS

Thinly sliced lemon quarters

Lemon zest

White cake glitter dust

1. Preheat your oven to 350°F and line 24 cupcake molds or muffin tins with paper liners.

2. Sift all the dry ingredients together in the mixing bowl. Add the milk, gin, lemon juice, oil and eggs to the dry ingredients and beat well until smooth and creamy. Using a large spoon, carefully fill each of the cupcake liners to about ¾-full. Bake for 17–20 minutes or until a skewer inserted into the center of the cupcake comes out clean. Leave to cool slightly for about 5 minutes before turning out onto a rack.

3. Whisk together all the ingredients for the glaze. While the cupcakes are cooling in the tins, poke several holes in the top of the cakes and soak the glaze mixture into the top (You should have enough to do each cupcake twice).

4. For the icing, cream the butter well in the electric mixer. Gradually add half of the confectioner's sugar until it is thoroughly combined. Alternate adding a little of the gin and tonic at a time with the rest of the confectioner's sugar until your icing looks thick enough to spread or pipe.

5. Ice the cupcakes, place a little lemon slice on top of each, sprinkle with lemon zest and dust with cake glitter.

Tip: A pinch of salt brings out the flavors in sweet baked goods. You may notice that all my recipes contain salt. Add a pinch to your icing as well for that extra depth of flavor.

Snowball cupcakes with advocaat

My mom isn't much of a drinker—the odd glass of hanepoot wine or a sweetish white wine once in a blue moon is about it. But I do remember that when I was quite young, she would really enjoy a Snowball on occasion, so I've made these especially for her.

A Snowball is a cocktail that is made from advocaat (an egg-nog type of liqueur) and lemonade.

3 cups cake flour

1½ cups sugar

4 t baking powder

1 t salt

2 T milk

½ cup advocaat

1 cup vegetable oil

4 large eggs

2 t lemon juice

Zest of 1 lemon

FILLING

½ cup cream (divide this into 2 x ¼ cups)

½ cup advocaat

5 T sugar

2 T cornstarch

2 egg yolks

1 whole egg

2 T butter

1 t vanilla extract

ICING

½ cup butter or margarine

2½ cups sifted confectioner's sugar

4 T advocaat

1 t lemon juice

DECORATION

Cream cake glitter dust

1. Preheat your oven to 350°F and line 24 cupcake molds or muffin tins with paper liners.
2. Sift all the dry ingredients together in a mixing bowl. Add the milk, advocaat, oil, eggs and lemon juice to the dry ingredients and beat well until smooth and creamy. Add the lemon zest and fold through. Using a large spoon, carefully fill each of the cupcake liners to about ¾-full. Bake for 17-20 minutes or until a skewer inserted into the center of the cupcake comes out clean. Leave to cool slightly for about 5 minutes before turning out onto a rack.
3. To make the filling, place cream, advocaat and sugar in a saucepan. Bring this mixture to the boil and then remove from the stove.
4. In a medium bowl, whisk the cornstarch with the other ¼ cup of cream and then beat in 2 egg yolks and 1 whole egg. Pour ⅓ of the boiling Advocaat mix into the egg mix but remember to keep whisking as you add this so that the eggs don't cook. Pour the mixture from the bowl into the hot advocaat mix in the saucepan in a thin stream whisking all the time again. Place the saucepan back on the heat and whisk constantly until the mixture reaches the consistency of very thick custard, remove from the heat and beat in the butter and the vanilla extract. Leave to one side to cool.

5. Using an apple-corer, small round cookie cutter or a knife, cut holes in the top of the cooled cupcakes about 1½-2cm deep. Remove the excess cake from the divots and keep the tops as lids. Spoon the cooled filling into the holes in the cupcakes, almost to the top and pop the little lids back on.
6. For the icing, cream the butter well in the electric mixer. Gradually add half of the confectioner's sugar until it is thoroughly combined. Alternate adding a little of the advocaat and lemon juice at a time with the rest of the confectioner's sugar until your icing looks thick enough to spread or pipe. Dust with a little cream cake glitter.

ALTERNATIVES:
♥ Any cream liqueur works well with this recipe—simply substitute for the advocaat.
♥ For a non-alcoholic version, use full cream milk instead of advocaat.

Tip: To bring butter to room temperature quickly, cut into small cubes and leave on a plate for about 15 minutes.

Highland milk punch

My mother-in-law is Scottish, so some time ago I came up with this recipe especially for her. Highland milk punch is actually a cocktail that contains Scotch whisky (not a favorite drink of mine) and Drambuie (which I love) and conjures up visions of stark Scottish Highlands, long-haired shaggy cows and country lanes lined with stone walls.

We lived in Scotland for a short while many years ago and I loved everything about the place except the weather. This drink would have been perfect on those cold, wet evenings! It is a warm eggy-milk cocktail dusted with cinnamon. My recipe recreates that fluffy, milky goodness with the warmth of the whisky coming through very subtly.

3 cups cake flour
1½ cups sugar
4 t baking powder
1 t salt
½ cup milk
⅓ cup Scotch whisky
3 T Drambuie
1 cup vegetable oil
4 large eggs
2 T vanilla extract

ICING
½ cup butter or margarine
2½ cups sifted confectioner's sugar
2 T Drambuie

DECORATIONS
Sprinkling of ground cinnamon
Bronze cake glitter dust

1. Preheat your oven to 350°F and line 24 cupcake molds or muffin tins with paper liners.
2. Sift all the dry ingredients together straight into the mixing bowl. Add the milk, whisky, Drambuie, oil, eggs and vanilla to the dry ingredients and beat well until smooth and creamy.
3. Using a large spoon, carefully fill each of the cupcake liners to about ¾-full. Bake for 17–20 minutes or until a skewer inserted into the center of the cupcake comes out clean. Leave to cool for about 5 minutes before turning out onto a rack.
4. For the icing, cream the butter well in the electric mixer. Gradually add half of the confectioner's sugar until it is thoroughly combined. Alternate adding a little of the Drambuie at a time
with the rest of the confectioner's sugar until your icing looks thick enough to spread or pipe.
5. Ice your cupcakes and sprinkle with a little ground cinnamon and dust with a little bronze cake glitter.

ALTERNATIVES:
♥ Mix equal quantities of dark rum and brandy in place of the whisky and Drambuie and dust with a little nutmeg in place of the cinnamon for a Tom & Jerry cupcake.

Tip: Be careful not to over-soften butter. Most recipes call for butter at room temperature and there's always the temptation to pop cold butter in the microwave to quickly soften it, but it's much better to cut the butter into small pieces and let it stand for 30–45 minutes to get the right consistency. Butter that's too soft won't cream properly; good creaming is essential to create light, fluffy cakes with a fine crumb, and fluffy, smooth icing.

Mai Tai

Many, many years ago we went on a family holiday to Hawaii. It was amazing! I was too young at the time to actually drink the alcoholic version of Mai Tais, but have made up for it since then!

Mai Tais are very refreshing but STRONG! They slide down very easily—just before you do—and these cupcakes are as potent. The Mai Tai syrup makes these cupcakes extra moist and gooey (that's a very technical term). The cream cheese icing isn't too sweet and adds to the refreshing element of this delicious cupcake.

3 cups cake flour
1½ cups sugar
4 t baking powder
1 t salt
⅓ cup milk
2 T light rum
2 T dark rum
3 T orange juice
3 T pineapple juice
1 cup vegetable oil
4 large eggs
2 t vanilla extract
1 T grenadine

SYRUP
6 T butter
¾ cup sugar
1 T lemon juice
1 T orange juice
Pinch of salt
¼ cup rum

ICING
250g cream cheese
3–4 T sifted confectioner's sugar
2 T orange juice

DECORATIONS
Maraschino/glazed cherries
Cake glitter dust

1. Preheat your oven to 350°F and line 24 cupcake molds or muffin tins with paper liners.

2. Sift all the dry ingredients together straight into the mixing bowl. Add the milk, rum, juice, oil, eggs and vanilla to the dry ingredients and beat well until smooth and creamy.

3. Spoon 1 cup of the mixture out of the bowl and add the grenadine to this. Place about 1 T of the grenadine mix into the bottom of the cupcake liners. Carefully spoon the rest of the batter into the liners on top of the grenadine mixture being careful not to mix the two flavors. Carefully fill each of the cupcake liners to about ¾–full. Bake for 17–20 minutes or until a skewer inserted into the center of the cupcake comes out clean. Leave to cool slightly for about 5 minutes before turning out onto a rack.

4. To make the syrup, melt the butter in a saucepan over a medium heat. Once melted, add the sugar and boil for 5 minutes, stirring occasionally. Turn off the heat and add the rest of the ingredients. Once all is incorporated, return to the heat for another minute. While the cupcakes are still warm, soak them with the syrup using a pastry brush.

5. To make the icing, cream the cream cheese in your mixer until soft. Mix in the orange juice and beat well again. Gradually add the confectioner's sugar to taste. Before decorating your cupcakes, make sure they have cooled completely. Ice your cupcakes and top with a cherry and cake glitter.

ALTERNATIVES:
♥ If you don't want your Mai Tai cupcakes to be quite so strong, you can substitute some of the alcohol with the same quantity of milk in the batter and a mix of lemon and orange juice in the syrup.

Tip: When creaming butter and sugar, get the mixture very pale yellow and fluffy—this will take about 5 minutes.

Fuzzy Navel

Back in the day, before kids and mortgages (we're talking the 90s here), we often used to go down to the Durban beach-front after work to meet up with the "Rent-a-Crowd." These perfect summer evenings were filled with fuzzy navels, sex-on-the-beach cocktails and B-52s. This recipe is dedicated to the "Rent-a-Crowd"—our family of party animals with whom we shared weekends and many other experiences that can't be reported in print …

I teamed this cupcake with sweet cream as it's lighter and more refreshing than regular buttercream. If this recipe is a bit too tame, you can always add another 2 tablespoons of vodka to make the Fuzzy Navel's big brother—the Hairy Navel.

3 cups cake flour

1½ cups sugar

4 t baking powder

1 t salt

½ cup milk

¼ cup peach schnapps

¼ cup orange juice
(freshly squeezed)

1 cup vegetable oil

4 large eggs

2 ripe peaches, finely diced and
tossed in 1 t cake flour

CREAM TOPPING

1 cup whipping cream

2 T sifted confectioner's sugar

1 T peach schnapps

1 T orange juice

DECORATIONS

Orange zest

Cake glitter dust

1. Preheat your oven to 350°F and line 24 cupcake molds or muffin tins with paper liners.

2. Sift all the dry ingredients together in a mixing bowl. Add the milk, schnapps, orange juice, oil and eggs to the dry ingredients and beat well until smooth and creamy.

3. Gently stir in the finely diced peaches by hand. Using a large spoon, carefully fill each of the cupcake liners to about ¾-full. Bake for 17–20 minutes or until a skewer inserted into the center of the cupcake comes out clean. Leave to cool slightly for about 5 minutes before turning out onto a rack.

4. To make the cream topping, place a large mixing bowl and beaters in the freezer for about 5–10 minutes. Once the bowl is chilled, pour cream into bowl and mix on high for about 1½ minutes or until the cream has thickened.

5. Once thick, stop the mixer and pour in the confectioner's sugar, schnapps and orange juice. Beat the cream, liquids and confectioner's sugar for about 2 minutes on high or until stiff peaks form.

6. Top your cupcakes with cream, sprinkle with a little orange zest and dust with cake glitter.

ALTERNATIVES:

♥ Add 2 T of vodka to the mix to make a stronger version called the Hairy Navel.

♥ To make a non-alcoholic version, substitute the peach schnapps for peach juice.

Tip: Ordinary margarine is not a suitable substitute for butter as it contains more water than butter and will throw off your ratios. If you are going to use margarine make sure that it is marked as baking margarine.

Glazed gingerbread with merlot icing

What is Christmas without gingerbread? We're used to gingerbread men and other ginger cookies but this variation on the holiday classic is super spicy, moist and delicious. The ginger liqueur glaze adds an extra dimension to the flavor and all this ginger teams very well with the merlot icing.

This recipe is a little more complicated than most of our other ones but well worth the effort!

1⅔ cups cake flour
1⅔ cups loosely packed brown sugar
1 t ground cinnamon
1 t ground nutmeg
1 t ground ginger
Pinch of ground cloves
4 t baking powder
1 t salt
½ cup vegetable oil
3 large eggs
¾ cup buttermilk
¾ cup molasses
4 T apple sauce
4 t puréed ginger

GLAZE
2½ cups sifted confectioner's sugar
4 T ginger liqueur
2 T lemon juice

ICING
1 cup merlot
½ cup butter or margarine
2½ cups sifted confectioner's sugar

DECORATIONS
Cake glitter dust

1. Preheat your oven to 350°F and line 24 cupcake molds or muffin tins with paper liners.
2. Sift all the dry ingredients together in a mixing bowl and mix with a paddle attachment until combined well. Slowly add the oil and eggs and mix thoroughly. Add the buttermilk, molasses, apple sauce and puréed ginger and beat well until smooth and creamy (about 2 minutes).
3. Fill the cupcake liners to ¾-full. Bake for 17–20 minutes or until a skewer inserted into the center of the cupcake comes out clean. Leave to cool slightly in the pans for about 5 minutes before turning out onto a rack.
4. To make the glaze, whisk together all the ingredients. While the cupcakes are cooling in the tins, poke several holes in the top of the cakes and soak the glaze mixture into the top. You should have enough to do each cupcake twice.
5. To make the icing, reduce the merlot over medium heat until you have about 2 T. Allow to cool. Cream the butter well in the electric mixer. Gradually add half of the confectioner's sugar until it is thoroughly combined. Alternate adding a little of the merlot reduction at a time with the rest of the confectioner's sugar until your icing looks thick enough to spread or pipe.
6. Ice the cupcakes and dust with cake glitter.

ALTERNATIVES:
♥ You can leave out the merlot if you don't like the idea of the tart wine flavor in the icing.

Tip: White margarine can be substituted for butter when making white icing. Yellow margarine or butter will result in a more yellow icing.

Springbokkie

Not too long ago, a friend of mine went through a bad patch—her husband asked her for a divorce and we moved her into her new home over the following three days. She has since then actually found that she's happier than she ever was and it was actually a blessing in disguise! Tania, this recipe is for you—you are my little "Springbokkie," bouncing back!

3 cups cake flour

1½ cups sugar

4 t baking powder

1 t salt

½ cup milk

½ cup Amarula Cream

1 cup vegetable oil

4 large eggs

2 T vanilla extract

FILLING

½ cup cream—divide this into 2 x ¼ cups

½ cup Peppermint Liqueur

5 T sugar

2 T cornstarch

2 egg yolks

1 whole egg

2 T butter

1 t vanilla extract

ICING

½ cup butter or margarine

2½ cups sifted confectioner's sugar

4 T Amarula

DECORATIONS

Green gel food coloring

Cream cake glitter dust

1. Preheat your oven to 350°F and line 24 cupcake molds or muffin tins with paper liners.

2. Sift all the dry ingredients together in a mixing bowl. Add the milk, Amarula, oil, eggs and vanilla to the dry ingredients and beat well until smooth and creamy. Using a large spoon, carefully fill each of the cupcake liners to about ¾-full. Bake for 17–20 minutes or until a skewer inserted into the center of the cupcake comes out clean. Leave to cool slightly for about 5 minutes before turning out onto a rack.

3. To make the cream filling, in a saucepan add ¼ cup of cream, peppermint liqueur and sugar. Bring to the boil and remove from the stove.

4. In a medium bowl, whisk the cornstarch with the other ¼ cup of cream and then beat in 2 egg yolks and 1 whole egg. Pour ⅓ of the boiling peppermint liqueur mix into the egg mix but remember to keep whisking as you add this so that the eggs don't cook. Pour the mixture from the bowl into the hot peppermint liqueur mix in the saucepan in a thin stream whisking all the time again. Place the saucepan back on the heat and whisk constantly until the mixture reaches the consistency of very thick custard, remove from the heat and beat in the butter and the vanilla extract. Leave to cool.

5. Using an apple-corer, small round cookie cutter or a knife, cut holes in the top of the cooled cupcakes about 1½–2cm deep. Remove the excess cake from the divots and keep the tops as lids. Spoon the filling into the holes and pop the little lids back on.

6. For the icing, cream the butter well in the electric mixer. Gradually add half of the confectioner's sugar until it is thoroughly combined. Alternate adding a little of the Amarula at a time with the rest of the confectioner's sugar until your icing looks thick enough to spread or pipe.

7. To get the green stripe in the icing, paint some gel food coloring in a stripe on the inside of the piping bag and then fill with icing. Do a test swirl before starting on the cakes. Dust the cupcakes with some cake glitter.

Tip: Be accurate with your sugar—too much can cause a dark crust (one of several possible causes); too little can cause too light a crust or tough texture.

Bushwacker

When I originally planned this book, I knew I had to dedicate a recipe to one of our oldest friends—Andrew. The Drew now lives in the Caribbean and when I told him about dedicating a cupcake to him (originally I thought the Painkiller), he told me that the Bushwacker was the one. No pressure! It has Baileys, Kahlúa, Amaretto, Vodka AND coconut rum!

3 cups cake flour

1½ cups sugar

4 t baking powder

1 t salt

½ cup coconut milk

¼ cup Bailey's Irish Cream

¼ cup Kahlúa

1 cup vegetable oil

4 large eggs

2 T light rum

AMARETTO-VODKA INFUSION

¼ cup amaretto

¼ cup vodka

ICING

½ cup butter or margarine

2½ cups sifted confectioner's sugar

1 t Baileys

1 t Kahlúa

1 t amaretto

DECORATIONS

Powdered nutmeg

Cake glitter dust

Coconut flakes (optional)

1. Preheat your oven to 350°F and line 24 cupcake molds or muffin tins with paper liners.

2. Sift all the dry ingredients together in a mixing bowl. Add the coconut milk, Baileys, Kahlúa, oil, eggs and rum to the dry ingredients and beat well until smooth and creamy. Using a large spoon, carefully fill each of the cupcake liners to about ¾-full. Bake for 17–20 minutes or until a skewer inserted into the center of the cupcake comes out clean. Leave to cool for about 5 minutes before turning out onto a rack.

3. Before the cakes cool down prick holes in the tops of the cakes and brush the amaretto-vodka mixture over the tops until it soaks into the cakes (about 2–3 dips with the pastry brush) without making them soggy.

4. To make the icing, cream the butter well in the electric mixer. Gradually add half of the confectioner's sugar until it is thoroughly combined. Alternate adding a little of the alcohol mix at a time with the rest of the confectioner's sugar until your icing looks thick enough to spread or pipe.

5. Ice your cupcakes and sprinkle with powdered nutmeg and a dusting of cake glitter. Add the coconut for an extra nutty flavor.

ALTERNATIVES:

♥ You can use regular milk instead of coconut milk if you don't want the coconut flavor. You can also use *lite* coconut milk if you're watching those calories!

Tip: Don't scoop flour out of the canister, essentially packing it down into the measuring cup, or tap the cup on the counter and then top off with more flour. Both of these methods result in too much flour being used. Always spoon flour lightly into dry measuring cups and then level with a knife. Never pack it in.

Pear, hazelnut & Frangelico

I met my friend Cheryl when we first arrived back in South Africa and I was looking for something to do; I joined a mosaic class at a craft shop in our local mall. Cheryl is also from Natal and we hit it off immediately. She has become like a sister and I can always rely on her for a level-headed approach to anything. We get together once a week still to try and work on our mosaics. Cheryl does a lot better than me as I tend to be busy with everything besides, but I grout her works of art with pleasure!

Pears are her favorite fruit and Frangelico is her favorite liqueur so the combination of the two makes this very special—just like my friend.

1 tin tinned pears in juice
½ cup Frangelico
3 cups cake flour
1½ cups sugar
4 t baking powder
1 t salt
½ cup milk
½ cup pear juice
1 cup vegetable oil
4 large eggs
2 t vanilla extract
1 cup chopped hazelnuts
   (reserve 2 T for decoration)

ICING

½ cup butter or margarine
2½ cups sifted confectioner's sugar
4 T Frangelico

DECORATIONS

2 T chopped hazelnuts
Cake glitter dust

1. Drain the pears and cut into 2cm chunks. Reserve the juice for the cake batter. Add the pears and the liqueur to a saucepan and bring to a simmer, poaching on medium to low heat for about 10 minutes being careful not to boil (steam should just start rising from the pot). Remove from heat and allow to cool in the saucepan (this allows the pears to soak up the hazelnut flavor). Do NOT drain.

2. Preheat your oven to 350°F and line 24 cupcake molds or muffin tins with paper liners.

3. Sift all the dry ingredients together in a mixing bowl. Add the milk, pear juice, oil, eggs and vanilla to the dry ingredients and beat well until smooth and creamy. Fill the cupcake liners to halfway.

4. Mix the chopped hazelnuts (keeping 2 T to one side for decoration) into the pear and Frangelico mixture. Spoon the pear-hazelnut mixture in the centers of your cake batter in the cupcake molds or muffin tins. Gently spoon more cake batter over the top with a teaspoon so that the pear is completely covered. Bake for 17–20 minutes or until a skewer inserted into the center of the cupcake comes out clean. Leave to cool for about 5 minutes before turning out onto a rack.

5. To make the icing, cream the butter well in the electric mixer. Gradually add half of the confectioner's sugar until it is thoroughly combined. Alternate adding a little of the Frangelico at a time with the rest of the confectioner's sugar until your icing looks thick enough to spread or pipe.

6. Ice the cupcakes, sprinkle the reserved chopped hazelnut on top of the piped icing and dust with a little cake glitter.

ALTERNATIVES:
♥ To make a non-alcoholic version, you can leave out the Frangelico and simply poach the pears in some of the juice from the tin. Use the pear juice in the icing instead of the alcohol as well.

Tip: Don't boil instead of simmer—simmering is when there is steam rising from the surface and a bubble or two breaks the surface every few seconds. Boiling is when there are bubbles rising vigorously.

Amaretto, lemon & thyme

I'm a great fan of fresh herbs and I love the lightness and simplicity of these cakes. They are more of an afternoon garden-party type recipe and need to be eaten the same day due to the fresh cream that is used instead of icing. I especially love the sandwich effect rather than the traditional icing on top.

I'm dedicating these cupcakes to my book club girls, who were my guinea pigs when I first tried this recipe. The cakes were a HUGE hit!

3 cups cake flour
4 t baking powder
1 t salt
1½ cups almond meal
2 cups sugar
6 large eggs
4 t lemon zest
¼ cup milk
¼ cup amaretto
1½ cup olive oil
4 t fresh thyme

FILLING

2 cups whipping cream
1 T lemon juice
2 T amaretto
¼ cup–½ cup honey depending on taste
1 t vanilla

DECORATIONS

Sprigs of fresh thyme
Confectioner's sugar for dusting (optional)

1. Preheat your oven to 350°F and line 24 cupcake molds or muffin tins with paper liners.

2. Sift the flour, baking powder and salt in a separate bowl and add the almond meal. Stir to combine these well.

3. In your electric mixer, add the sugar, eggs and lemon zest and beat at a medium to medium–high speed until these are pale and fluffy. Add the milk, amaretto and the olive oil and mix well. Add the dry ingredients and mix until just combined. Fill the cupcake liners to about ⅔-full and place a sprig of fresh thyme on top for decoration. Bake for 17–20 minutes or until a skewer inserted into the center of the cupcake comes out clean. Leave to cool slightly for about 5 minutes before turning out onto a rack.

4. To make the cream filling, whip the cream in a mixer until it just begins to thicken. Add the lemon juice, amaretto and honey (to taste) and continue to beat until soft peaks begin to form.

5. If you've used cupcake liners, peel the wrappers gently off the cool cupcakes and slice in half. Top the bottom halves with a spoon of cream and place the tops back like sandwiches. Dust with a little confectioner's sugar (optional).

ALTERNATIVES:
♥ If you can't find almond meal, you can chop almonds to a fine powder in a blender.

Tip: Don't skip the sifting! This step helps to add air and ensures that all dry ingredients are properly combined. If you don't have a sieve, you can use a wire mesh strainer.

Black forest trifle

Last Christmas was the first time that we spent the day with friends and not family and everyone pitched in with regard to the menu. I decided that since Christmas trifle is an institution, I needed to make a special cupcake for the occasion. This is my cupcake creation; I hope this tradition will live on!

2 cups flour

1 t salt

1 t baking powder

2 t baking soda

¾ cup unsweetened cocoa powder

2 cups sugar

1 cup vegetable oil

1 cup strong, hot coffee

1 cup milk

2 large eggs

1 t vanilla extract

JELLY FILLING

1 tin tinned pitted black cherries in syrup, drained and syrup reserved

1 cup cherry liqueur or kirschwasser

2 t agar-agar powder

CREAM FILLING

½ cup cream—divide this into 2 x ¼ cups

½ cup cherry liqueur or kirschwasser

5 T sugar

2 T cornstarch

2 egg yolks

1 whole egg

2 T butter

1 t vanilla extract

DECORATIONS

Fresh whipped cream for topping

Maraschino/glazed cherries

1. Preheat your oven to 350°F and line 24 cupcake molds or muffin tins with paper liners.
2. Sift all the dry ingredients together. Add oil, coffee and milk and mix on medium speed for 2 minutes. Add eggs and vanilla extract and beat for 2 more minutes. Using a large spoon, carefully fill each of the cupcake liners to about ⅔-full. Bake for 17–20 minutes or until a skewer inserted into the center of the cupcake comes out clean. Leave to cool slightly for about 5 minutes before turning out onto a rack. Once cooled, chill in the fridge for about 10 minutes.
3. Using an apple-corer, small round cookie cutter or a knife, cut holes in the top of the cooled cupcakes about 1½–2cm deep. Remove the excess cake from the divots and keep the tops as lids. Place in the fridge to chill so that the jelly will set immediately when it is poured into the cupcakes.
4. To make the jelly, mix the agar–agar powder with the reserved cherry syrup and the cherry liqueur in a saucepan and bring to the boil, making sure that all the agar powder is dissolved. Leave to one side to cool slightly. (Don't allow the agar jelly to cool completely as it sets at room temperature.) Pour enough jelly into the chilled cupcakes to fill the holes halfway and allow to set.
5. To make the cream filling, place the cream, cherry liqueur/kirschwasser and sugar in a saucepan. Bring the mixture to the boil and remove from the stove.
6. In a medium bowl, whisk the cornstarch with the other ¼ cup of cream and then beat in the 2 egg yolks and 1 whole egg. Pour ⅓ of the boiling cherry liqueur/kirschwasser mix into the egg mix but remember to keep whisking as you add this so that the eggs don't cook. Pour the mixture from the bowl into the hot cherry liqueur/kirschwasser mix in the saucepan in a thin stream whisking all the time again. Place the saucepan back on the heat and whisk constantly until the mixture reaches the consistency of very thick custard, remove from the heat and beat in the butter and the vanilla extract. Leave to one side to cool.
7. Spoon the cooled cream filling into the holes in the cupcakes filling them almost to the top and pop the little lids back on. Pipe fresh whipped cream on top of each cupcake and place a cherry on top, then sprinkle with grated chocolate.

ALTERNATIVES:
♥ For a non-alcoholic version, you can leave out the cherry liqueur and simply use the cherry juice from the tin.

Tip: Use measuring spoons, not eating utensils, to measure small amounts. Don't guess. Use the exact measurements and level off spoons with a straight edge spatula or knife.

Raspberry chardonnay

This recipe came into being all on its own and was the result of happy experimentation. The gorgeous, fresh summer raspberries were just too tempting to pass up and it didn't take too long to team these fresh, tart creations with summer chardonnay.

This recipe is dedicated to the glorious Cape summer and is a celebration of some of its best flavors!

1 tin tinned raspberries or mixed berries in syrup
3 cups cake flour
1½ cups sugar
4 t baking powder
1 t salt
1 cup chardonnay
1 cup apple sauce
4 large eggs
2 t vanilla extract

SYRUP

Syrup from the tin of berries
1 cup chardonnay

ICING

½ cup butter or margarine
2½ cups sifted confectioner's sugar
1 cup chardonnay
raspberry syrup from tin

DECORATIONS

3 T reduced raspberry chardonnay syrup
Fresh raspberries
Cake glitter dust

1. Drain the raspberries and reserve the juice for the raspberry-chardonnay syrup.
2. Preheat your oven to 350°F and line 24 cupcake molds or muffin tins with paper liners.
3. Sift all the dry ingredients together in a mixing bowl. Add the chardonnay, apple sauce, eggs and vanilla to the dry ingredients and beat well until smooth and creamy. Fold the well-drained berries gently into the batter mix.
4. Fill the cupcake liners to just over halfway. Bake for 17-20 minutes or until a skewer inserted into the center of the cupcake comes out clean. Leave to cool for about 5 minutes before turning out onto a rack.
5. To make the syrup, use the liquid from the tinned berries and add 1 cup of chardonnay and reduce over a high heat until you have about ¼ cup of thick glaze. If necessary, add a little cornstarch to thicken slightly and cook well.
6. For the icing, cream the butter well in the electric mixer. Gradually add half of the confectioner's sugar until it is thoroughly combined. Alternate adding a little of the raspberry-chardonnay reduction at a time with the rest of the sugar until your icing looks thick enough to spread or pipe.

7. Ice your cupcakes and drizzle the remaining raspberry-chardonnay reduction over the top. Finish it off with a fresh raspberry and a sprinkling of cake glitter.

ALTERNATIVES:
♥ You can add butter or oil in place of the apple sauce but the apple drastically cuts the fat content.
♥ Add milk in place of the char-donnay for a sober version and leave out the chardonnay in the syrup.

Tips: Generally, the cake batter should fill the pans or cups by at least ½ and not more than ⅔, unless otherwise instructed.

B-52

Thinking back to the shooters we used to enjoy when we were younger, one that I especially remember is the B-52—a layered shot of Kahlúa, Irish Cream and Grand Marnier. If you were really brave (or stupid), you would try the Flaming B-52—where the alcohol on top produces a lovely blue flame. I know of quite a few of our friends who suffered from burns for days afterwards!

These cupcakes are very much like the shooters—they have a Kahlúa cake base, a Baileys cream filling, are topped with a Grand Marnier icing and are gone in just one bite!

3 cups cake flour

1½ cups sugar

4 t baking powder

1 t coffee powder

1 t salt

½ cup milk

½ cup Kahlúa

1 cup vegetable oil

4 large eggs

1 t vanilla extract

CREAM FILLING

1 cup cream—divide this into
   2 x ½ cups

1 cup Baileys

⅔ cup sugar

4 t cornstarch

2 egg yolks

1 whole egg

2 T butter

1 t vanilla extract

ICING

½ cup butter or margarine

2½ cups sifted confectioner's sugar

2 T Grand Marnier liqueur

DECORATIONS

Cake glitter dust

Note: I've made 48 mini cupcakes, so you can pop the whole cupcake in your mouth, just like you would the shot!

1. Preheat your oven to 350°F and line 48 small (or 24 regular) cupcake molds or muffin tins with paper liners.
2. Sift all the dry ingredients together in a mixing bowl. Add the milk, Kahlúa, oil, eggs and vanilla to the dry ingredients and beat well until smooth and creamy.
3. Fill the cupcake liners to halfway. Bake for 17–20 minutes for regular cupcakes or 12–15 minutes for mini cupcakes or until a skewer inserted into the center of the cupcake comes out clean. Leave to cool slightly for about 5 minutes before turning out onto a rack.
4. To make the cream filling, add ½ cup of cream, Baileys and sugar in a saucepan. Bring to the boil and remove from the heat.
5. In a medium bowl, whisk the cornstarch with the other ½ cup of cream and then beat in the 2 egg yolks and 1 whole egg. Pour ⅓ of the boiling Baileys mixture into the egg mix but remember to keep whisking as you add this so that the eggs don't cook. Pour the mixture from the bowl into the hot Baileys mix in the saucepan in a thin stream whisking all the time. Place the saucepan back on the heat and whisk constantly until the mixture reaches the consistency of very thick custard. Remove from the heat and beat in the butter and the vanilla extract. Leave to one side to cool.
6. Using an apple-corer, small round cookie cutter or a knife, cut holes in the top of the cooled cupcakes about 1½–2cm deep. Remove the excess cake from the divots and keep the tops as lids. Spoon the cooled cream filling into the holes in the cupcakes and pop the little lids back on.
7. For the icing, cream the butter well in the electric mixer. Gradually add half of the confectioner's sugar until it is thoroughly combined. Alternate adding a little of the Grand Marnier at a time with the rest of the confectioner's sugar until your icing looks thick enough to spread or pipe.
8. Ice the cupcakes and dust with a little gold cake glitter.

ALTERNATIVES:
♥ Substitute the Grand Marnier for vodka and you have a Mudslide cocktail cupcake.

Tip: If you're making mini cupcakes, don't worry about replacing the lids. The icing will cover the filling.

Glühwein

There are certain flavors that go with Christmas and even if it's over 86° outside, glühwein (mulled wine) is definitely one of them. We've even attempted to drink it chilled and it's actually very good! Every year, my brother-in-law makes up a big batch of his famous glühwein. This year I decided to return the favor and make a cupcake version especially for him. Graham—I hope this measures up and starts a new family tradition!

2 cups flour

1 t salt

1 t baking powder

2 t baking soda

¾ cup unsweetened cocoa powder

1 cup sugar

1 cup brown sugar

1 t ground cinnamon

½ t ground cloves

½ t ground nutmeg

1 cup vegetable oil

1½ cups red wine

½ cup freshly squeezed orange juice

Zest of 1 orange

2 large eggs

1 t vanilla extract

ICING

1 cup full-fat cream-cheese

½ cup sifted confectioner's sugar

1 t ground cinnamon

CRYSTALLIZED GRAPES

Egg whites

Grapes

Caster sugar

DECORATIONS

24 crystallized grapes

Cake glitter

1. Preheat your oven to 350°F and line 24 cupcake molds or muffin tins with paper liners.

2. Sift all the dry ingredients together. Add oil, red wine, orange juice and zest and mix on medium speed for 2 minutes. Scrape the bottom of the mixing bowl with a spatula to make sure all ingredients are combined. Add eggs and vanilla extract and beat for 2 more minutes.

3. Using a large spoon, carefully fill each of the cupcake liners to about ⅔-full. Be careful not to over-fill the cups as this cake rises quite a bit. Bake for 17–20 minutes or until a skewer inserted into the center of the cupcake comes out clean. Leave to cool slightly for about 5 minutes before turning out onto a rack.

4. To make the icing, cream the cream cheese well. Gradually add half of the confectioner's sugar until it is thoroughly combined. Add the cinnamon with the rest of the sugar until your icing looks thick enough to spread or pipe.

5. To make the crystallized grapes, dip each grape in egg white and roll in caster sugar until well coated. Set to one side and allow to dry.

6. Ice the cupcakes, dust each cupcake with a little cake glitter and pop a crystallized grape on top.

ALTERNATIVES:

♥ If you don't have ground cloves and nutmeg, you can substitute these spices for 1 t (5ml) of ground allspice.

Tip: Always wait for your oven to reach the required temperature before you put your cupcakes in.

Milk stout with white chocolate liqueur icing

While doing research for this book, one recipe popped up over and over again: Guinness cupcakes with Baileys icing. The flavor combination intrigued me as there are very few beer cupcake recipes. As an alternative to Baileys, I had the option of Amarula or Cape Velvet but Amarula already featured prominently in a lot of recipes so I experimented with something completely different. This flavor combination was a HUGE success with the yeasty tones of the stout complemented perfectly by the sweet Milky Bar flavor of the icing.

2 cups cake flour
1 t salt
1 t baking powder
2 T baking soda
¾ cup unsweetened cocoa powder
2 cups sugar
1 cup vegetable oil
1 cup Castle milk stout
½ cup coffee
½ cup milk
2 large eggs
1 t vanilla extract

ICING

½ cup butter or margarine
3½ cups sifted confectioner's sugar
6 T McDonnell's Irish White
  Chocolate Cream Liqueur

DECORATIONS

White chocolate curls
Cake glitter dust

1. Preheat your oven to 350°F and line 24 cupcake molds or muffin tins with paper liners.
2. Sift all the dry ingredients together. Add oil, milk stout, coffee and milk and mix on medium speed for 2 minutes. Scrape the bottom of the mixing bowl with a spatula to make sure all ingredients are combined. Add eggs and vanilla extract and beat for 2 more minutes.
3. Using a large spoon, carefully fill each of the cupcake liners to about ⅔-full. Be careful not to over-fill the cups as this cake rises quite a bit. Bake for 17–20 minutes or until a skewer inserted into the center of the cupcake comes out clean. Leave to cool slightly for about 5 minutes before turning out onto a rack.
4. To make the icing, cream the butter well in the electric mixer. Gradually add half of the confectioner's sugar until it is thoroughly combined. Alternate adding a little of the white chocolate liqueur at a time with the rest of the sugar until your icing looks thick enough to spread or pipe. Sprinkle the white chocolate curls on top of the piped icing and dust with a little cake glitter.

ALTERNATIVES:
♥ If the white chocolate doesn't appeal, use any cream liqueur. Try Baileys, Cape Velvet or for something really different—Strawberry Lips!

Tip: Know your oven! Ideally, every oven set to 350°F should heat to 350°F. Many ovens don't, including expensive ones, and some change their behavior over time. Use a separate oven thermometer for an accurate temperature reading.

Milk stout & gingerbread

With the previous milk stout recipe, the chocolate hid quite a bit of the stout flavor and I wanted to do a cleaner version for the beer purists out there. I was also looking for an alternative to plain old gingerbread and the combination of the two ingredients seemed like a match made in heaven!

The dark stout gives the cupcakes a very odd color—not quite vanilla but not chocolate—it's a malty color which, as we eat with our eyes first, makes you start salivating almost immediately. I teamed this recipe with a lemon icing as this complements the earthy spice tones of the malt and ginger.

3 cups cake flour

1 cup sugar

½ cup molasses

4 t baking powder

1 t salt

2 t ground ginger

1 t ground cinnamon

1 t ground cloves

1 cup Castle milk stout

1 cup oil

4 large eggs

2 t vanilla extract

½ cup finely chopped candied ginger

ICING

½ cup butter or margarine

2½ cups sifted confectioner's sugar

2 T lemon juice

DECORATIONS

2 T chopped candied ginger

Cake glitter dust

1. Preheat your oven to 350°F and line 24 cupcake molds or muffin tins with paper liners.

2. Sift all the dry ingredients together straight into the mixing bowl. Add the milk stout, oil, eggs and vanilla to the dry ingredients and beat well until smooth and creamy. Mix the chopped ginger into the batter.

3. Using a large spoon, carefully fill each of the cupcake liners to about ⅔-full. Be careful not to over-fill the cups as this cake rises quite a bit. Bake for 17–20 minutes or until a skewer inserted into the center of the cupcake comes out clean. Leave to cool slightly for about 5 minutes before turning out onto a rack.

4. To make the icing, cream the butter well in the electric mixer. Gradually add half of the confectioner's sugar until it is thoroughly combined. Alternate adding a little of the lemon juice at a time with the rest of the confectioner's sugar until your icing looks thick enough to spread or pipe.

5. Ice the cupcakes, sprinkle the reserved chopped ginger on top of the piped icing and dust with a little cake glitter.

ALTERNATIVES:

♥ You can substitute the stout with a cup of milk to make a non-alcoholic version of these cupcakes.

Tip: Be aware of hot spots in your oven. If you've produced cake layers with wavy rather than flat tops, hot spots are the problem. You can do the bread test. Arrange bread slices to cover the middle oven rack. Bake at 350°F for a few minutes, and see which slices get singed—their location marks your oven's hot spot(s). If you know you have a hot spot in, say, the back left corner, avoid putting pans in that location, or rotate accordingly.

Chocolate & amaretto

My younger son loves Nutella more than anything, the inspiration for this recipe came from him. I found a Nutella brownie recipe in a magazine that worked well and I thought why not exchange the hazelnut flavor for almonds, which I think smell even better than vanilla when baking. So, in order to widen taste horizons, this is dedicated to Connor who, although shouldn't be eating these (as he's still underage), I hope will enjoy them in a couple of years.

1½ cups flour
½ cup almond flour or finely ground almonds
1 t salt
1 t baking powder
2 t baking soda
¾ cup unsweetened cocoa powder
2 cups sugar
1 cup vegetable oil
1 cup strong, hot coffee
½ cup coconut milk
½ cup amaretto
2 large eggs
1 t vanilla extract

ICING

½ cup butter or margarine
2½ cups sifted confectioner's sugar
4 T amaretto

DECORATION

2 T chopped or flaked almonds
Cake glitter dust

1. Preheat your oven to 350°F and line 24 cupcake molds or muffin tins with paper liners.
2. Sift all the dry ingredients together. Add oil, coffee and milk and mix on medium speed for 2 minutes. Scrape the bottom of the mixing bowl with a spatula to make sure all ingredients are combined. Add eggs and vanilla extract and beat for 2 more minutes.
3. Using a large spoon, carefully fill each of the cupcake liners to about ⅔-full. Be careful not to over-fill the cups as this cake rises quite a bit. Bake for 17–20 minutes or until a skewer inserted into the center of the cupcake comes out clean. Leave to cool slightly for about 5 minutes before turning out onto a rack.
4. To make the icing, cream the butter well in the electric mixer. Gradually add half of the confectioner's sugar until it is thoroughly combined. Alternate adding a little of the amaretto at a time with the rest of the sugar until your icing looks thick enough to spread or pipe.
5. Ice the cupcakes, sprinkle the reserved chopped almonds on top of the piped icing and dust with a little gold cake glitter.

ALTERNATIVES:
♥ You can substitute the amaretto for Frangelico and the almonds for hazelnuts if you prefer a classic Nutella flavor.

Tip: If necessary, rotate cupcakes to allow them to rise evenly.

Tiramisu

Whenever we go out to dinner and tiramisu is on the menu, my husband makes a beeline for this scrumptious dessert. Although he doesn't have much of a sweet tooth, this is his favorite, after milk tart. Having had so much support and encouragement from him over the twenty years that we've been married, I couldn't help but include this recipe for him. Ken, thank you for always being there for me and for putting up with being called Mr. Cupcake.

Traditional tiramisu is made with marsala wine, however, I've adjusted the recipe to use Kahlúa, which makes very little difference to the taste.

3 cups cake flour

1½ cups sugar

4 t baking powder

1 t salt

1 cup milk

1 cup vegetable oil

4 large eggs

2 T vanilla extract

SYRUP

½ cup strong, hot coffee or espresso

3 T Kahlúa

¼ cup confectioner's sugar

ICING

1 cup heavy cream

1 cup mascarpone cheese (room temperature)

½ cup sifted confectioner's sugar

DECORATION

Cocoa powder

1. Preheat your oven to 350°F and line 24 cupcake molds or muffin tins with paper liners.

2. Sift all the dry ingredients together straight into the mixing bowl. Add the milk, oil, eggs and vanilla to the dry ingredients and beat well until smooth and creamy.

3. Using a large spoon, carefully fill each of the cupcake liners to about ⅔-full. Be careful not to over-fill the cups as this cake rises quite a bit. Bake for 17-20 minutes or until a skewer inserted into the center of the cupcake comes out clean. Leave to cool slightly for about 5 minutes before turning out onto a rack.

4. To make the syrup, heat all the ingredients in a saucepan, stirring until the sugar has dissolved; allow to cool. Brush the tops of the cupcakes with the Kahlúa syrup. Repeat until all the syrup has been soaked into the cakes. Allow the syrup to further absorb for another 30 minutes.

5. To make the icing, whisk the heavy cream until stiff peaks form (be careful not to overbeat, or cream will be grainy), preferably with an electric mixer on a medium speed setting.

6. In another bowl, whisk together mascarpone and confectioner's sugar until smooth. Gently fold whipped cream into mascarpone mixture until completely incorporated.

7. Dollop the icing onto the cupcakes and refrigerate overnight in an airtight container. Dust generously with cocoa powder just before serving.

ALTERNATIVES:
- ♥ Rum can also be used instead of Kahlúa or you can leave out the Kahlúa altogether for non-alcoholic tiramisu.

Tip: If you have an electric, fan-assisted oven, then the temperature should be fairly constant and timings as given in the recipes will be correct. If you have a gas oven that heats from the bottom only, you may find that your cupcakes cook unevenly or overflow. This can be rectified by placing a baking tray beneath the cupcake pan filled with a ½ cm of water. This keeps the bottoms cool while the rest of the cake is heating up and they will then bake evenly with nice round tops. You may need to add 3-5 minutes to the baking time though.

Chocolate, coffee & pinotage

This recipe works well with any red wine that you may have on hand. I used pinotage because it is full-bodied and has strong chocolate and coffee undertones. The next best alternative, in my opinion, would be merlot, but I'm pretty sure that whatever red wine you use, these cupcakes will be just as delicious!

2 cups flour

1 t salt

1 t baking powder

2 t baking soda

¾ cup unsweetened cocoa powder

2 cups sugar

1 cup vegetable oil

½ cup strong, hot coffee

1½ cups pinotage

2 large eggs

1 t vanilla extract

ICING

1 cup pinotage reduced to 2 T

½ cup butter or margarine

2½ cups sifted confectioner's sugar

¼ cup unsweetened cocoa powder

DECORATIONS

2 T chopped or grated dark chocolate

Cake glitter dust

1. Preheat your oven to 350°F and line 24 cupcake molds or muffin tins with paper liners.

2. Sift all the dry ingredients together. Add oil, coffee and pinotage and mix on medium speed for 2 minutes. Scrape the bottom of the mixing bowl with a spatula to make sure all ingredients are combined. Add eggs and vanilla extract and beat for 2 more minutes.

3. Using a large spoon, carefully fill each of the cupcake liners to about ⅔-full. Be careful not to over-fill the cups as this cake rises quite a bit. Bake for 17–20 minutes or until a skewer inserted into the center of the cupcake comes out clean. Leave to cool slightly for about 5 minutes before turning out onto a rack.

4. For the icing, reduce the pinotage to about 2 T n a saucepan over medium heat and allow to cool.

5. Cream the butter well in the electric mixer. Gradually add half of the confectioner's sugar and all of the cocoa powder until everything is thoroughly combined. Alternate adding a little of the pinotage reduction at a time with the rest of the confectioner's sugar until your icing looks thick enough to spread or pipe.

6. Ice the cupcakes, sprinkle the reserved chopped dark chocolate on top of the piped icing and dust with a little cake glitter.

Tip: Always use the middle rack and don't be tempted to overcrowd your oven if you have a few batches of cupcakes to bake.

Tia Maria & toffee

Tia Maria is a coffee liqueur that originated in Jamaica and isn't as sweet as Kahlúa. The strong coffee flavor in the cake isn't diluted by other flavors such as chocolate and pairs beautifully with the toffee on top. The secret surprise of the toffee cream in the center makes this cupcake a real hit!

As these cupcakes have a fresh cream filling, they need to be kept refrigerated until serving.

3 cups cake flour

1½ cups sugar

4 t baking powder

1 t salt

2 t instant coffee powder

½ cup strong coffee or espresso

½ cup Tia Maria

1 cup vegetable oil

4 large eggs

2 t toffee essence

CREAM FILLING

1 cup heavy cream

2 T caster sugar

½ cup chopped toffee bits
   (Werther's)

ICING

½ cup butter or margarine

2½ cups sifted confectioner's sugar

¼ cup Caramel Treat

3 T toffee vodka

DECORATIONS

2 T chopped toffee bits (Werther's)

Cake glitter dust

1. Preheat your oven to 350°F and line 24 cupcake molds or muffin tins with paper liners.

2. Sift all the dry ingredients. Add the coffee, Tia Maria, oil, eggs and toffee essence to the dry ingredients and beat well until smooth and creamy.

3. Fill the cupcake liners to halfway and bake for 17–20 minutes or until a skewer inserted into the center of the cupcake comes out clean. Leave to cool slightly for about 5 minutes before turning out onto a rack.

4. To make the filling, whip the cream and caster sugar until stiff and smooth and fold in the toffee bits. When the cupcakes are cool, carve out a cone-shaped hole and fill this with the toffee cream.

5. For the icing, cream the butter well in the electric mixer. Gradually add half of the confectioner's sugar until it is thoroughly combined. Alternate adding a little of the toffee vodka and Caramel Treat at a time with the rest of the confectioner's sugar until your icing looks thick enough to spread or pipe. Spread or pipe your icing directly onto the hole with the cream filling.

6. Sprinkle the chopped toffee pieces on top of the piped icing and dust with a little cake glitter, coffee or cocoa powder.

ALTERNATIVES:

♥ You can use Kahlúa or Mokador instead of Tia Maria.

♥ For a non-alcoholic version, use a sweet chocolate syrup instead of the Tia Maria in the batter, and milk instead of vodka for the icing. You can make your own coffee syrup with ½ cup (125ml) water, 1 T (15ml) sugar and 2 t (10ml) instant coffee.

Mojitos

Cakes don't get any fresher than this and I don't mean in terms of coming straight out of the oven! When I first heard of this recipe, I had visions of the cupcakes tasting a bit like toothpaste but I was very, very wrong! They're not too sweet and the cream cheese icing adds another cool and refreshing element to these amazing cakes.

½ cup milk

½ cup finely chopped fresh mint leaves

3 cups cake flour

1½ cups sugar

4 t baking powder

1 t salt

½ cup rum

1 cup vegetable oil

4 large eggs

2 t vanilla extract

ICING

1 cup full-fat cream-cheese

1 T lime juice

1 T lime zest

¼ cup finely chopped mint

½ cup sifted confectioner's sugar

DECORATIONS

Mint leaves

Cake glitter dust or white sparkle sugar crystals

1. Preheat your oven to 350°F and line 24 cupcake molds or muffin tins with paper liners.
2. Combine the milk and mint in a saucepan and simmer until hot—but NOT boiling. Remove from the heat and allow to steep for 10–15 minutes. Set aside to cool.
3. Sift all the dry ingredients together straight into the mixing bowl. Add the milk–mint infusion, rum, oil, eggs and vanilla to the dry ingredients and beat well until smooth and creamy.
4. Fill the cupcake liners to halfway and bake for 17–20 minutes or until a skewer inserted into the center of the cupcake comes out clean. Leave to cool for about 5 minutes before turning out onto a rack.
5. To make the icing, cream the cream cheese in your mixer until soft. Mix in the lime juice, zest and chopped mint and beat well again. Gradually add the confectioner's sugar to taste.
6. Decorate with a fresh mint leaf and dust with a little cake glitter.

Tip: Mint leaves blacken when left overnight, so decorate these cupcakes just before serving.

Sambuca–Kahlúa shot

Daniel has been a friend of ours ever since we can remember—he was my husband's housemate for years and was even his best man at our wedding. One thing about Daniel is that he always looked after us very well: before we could go out for the evening he made sure we'd taken our "cough syrup"—a shot of sambuca which would see us on our way. Now that we're all older and wiser I've made this tribute to Danny-Boy and hope we'll enjoy these as much as the "cough syrup."

2 cups flour
1 t salt
1 t baking powder
2 t baking soda
¾ cup unsweetened cocoa powder
2 cups sugar
1 cup vegetable oil
1 cup strong, hot coffee
1 cup sambuca
2 large eggs
1 t vanilla extract

GANACHE
1 cup chopped dark chocolate
¾ cup heavy cream
2 T butter
2 T Kahlúa
2 T sambuca

DECORATIONS
2 chocolate-covered coffee beans
  for each cupcake
Cake glitter dust

Note: I made 48 mini cupcakes, but you could make 24 regular ones.

1. Preheat your oven to 350°F and line 24/48 cupcake molds or muffin tins with paper liners.
2. Sift all the dry ingredients together. Add oil, coffee and sambuca and mix on medium speed for 2 minutes. Scrape the bottom of the mixing bowl with a spatula to make sure all ingredients are combined. Add eggs and vanilla extract and beat for 2 more minutes.
3. Fill the cupcake liners to halfway. Bake for 17–20 minutes for regular cupcakes or 12–15 minutes for mini cupcakes or until a skewer inserted into the center of the cupcake comes out clean. Leave to cool slightly for about 5 minutes before turning out onto a rack.
4. To make the ganache, place the chopped chocolate in a heatproof bowl. Heat the cream in a saucepan until just boiling and then pour over the chocolate. Cover and allow to stand for 2 minutes for the chocolate to soften. Uncover and stir with a whisk until smooth and silky. Stir in butter until fully combined and then add the Kahlúa and sambuca and stir well again.

5. The ganache will thicken as it cools. Dip the mini cupcakes in the slightly cooled ganache and allow to set completely on a wire rack or pour ganache over the top of regular cupcakes and allow to set on a wire rack. Top with 2 chocolate covered espresso beans and dust with a little cake glitter.

ALTERNATIVES:
♥ Try a pinch of paprika in the cake batter for an extra chilli zing.

Tip: Taste as you go—even though baking is a carefully controlled process, a million things could affect the outcome. Everything from the freshness of the ingredients, their temperature before use, to humidity and climate. Your palate is the ultimate control factor so test as you go.

Jack Daniel's & dark chocolate

These amazing cupcakes are incredibly masculine—they are perfect for poker nights or Father's day. Chocolate on chocolate and still more chocolate with a rich, dark Jack Daniel's bomb in the center!

2 cups flour
1 t salt
1 t baking powder
2 t baking soda
¾ cup unsweetened cocoa powder
2 cups sugar
1 cup vegetable oil
½ cup very strong, hot coffee
½ cup Jack Daniel's
1 cup buttermilk
2 large eggs
1 t vanilla extract

GANACHE
1 cup chopped dark chocolate
¾ cup heavy cream
2 T butter
4 T Jack Daniel's

ICING
½ cup butter or margarine
2½ cups sifted confectioner's sugar
½ cup cocoa powder
4 T Jack Daniels

DECORATIONS
Grated dark chocolate
Cake glitter dust

1. Preheat your oven to 350°F and line 24 cupcake molds or muffin tins with paper liners.
2. Sift all the dry ingredients together. Add oil, coffee, Jack Daniels and buttermilk and mix on medium speed for 2 minutes. Scrape the bottom of the mixing bowl with a spatula to make sure all ingredients are combined. Add eggs and vanilla extract and beat for 2 more minutes.
3. Fill the cupcake liners to halfway and bake for 17–20 minutes or until a skewer inserted into the center of the cupcake comes out clean. Leave to cool slightly for about 5 minutes before turning out onto a rack.
4. To make the ganache, place the chopped chocolate in a heatproof bowl. Heat the cream in a saucepan until just boiling and then pour over the chocolate. Cover and allow to stand for 2 minutes for the chocolate to soften. Uncover and stir with a whisk until smooth and silky. Stir in butter until fully combined and then add the Jack Daniels and stir well again. The ganache will thicken as it cools.
5. Using an apple-corer, small round cookie cutter or a knife, cut holes in the top of the cooled cupcakes about 1½–2cm deep. Remove the excess cake from the divots and keep the tops as lids. Spoon the ganache into a plastic sandwich bag and twist the top to seal. Cut off the tip of one of the corners and pipe the ganache into the holes in the cupcakes. Pop the lids back on the cupcakes.

6. For the icing, cream the butter well in the electric mixer. Gradually add half of the confectioner's sugar and all of the cocoa powder until everything is thoroughly combined. Alternate adding a little of the Jack Daniel's at a time with the rest of the confectioner's sugar until your icing looks thick enough to spread or pipe.
7. Ice the cupcakes, sprinkle with grated dark chocolate on top of the piped icing and dust with a little cake glitter.

ALTERNATIVES:
♥ This is a very versatile recipe and any spirits will work well.

Tip: When folding, you should always add the lighter of the two mixtures on top, using a gentle folding motion to avoid deflating the batter.

Pink port

When I had the idea of creating a sweet-wine cupcake, the person who kept popping into my mind was one of my very dearest friends: Tasha is a beauty therapist, was my bridesmaid, and we've been through many, many experiences together. I wanted to make these cakes as sweet and beautiful as she is.

These are a white version of red velvet cupcakes. The tartness and slight acidity of the buttermilk and vinegar balance beautifully with the sweetness of the wine. The pink port cream–cheese icing is the perfect finish.

2¼ cups cake flour

1 t baking soda

1 t baking powder

1 t salt

1¾ cups sugar

1 cup vegetable oil

2 large eggs

½ cup buttermilk

2 t vanilla extract

1 t white distilled vinegar

1 cup pink port

ICING

1 cup full-fat cream-cheese

2 T pink port

½ cup sifted confectioner's sugar

DECORATIONS

Cake glitter dust

1. Preheat your oven to 350°F and line 24 cupcake molds or muffin tins with paper liners.
2. In a medium bowl, sift together the flour, baking soda (baking soda), baking powder and salt.
3. In another bowl, combine the sugar and oil. Add in the eggs, buttermilk, vanilla, vinegar and port. Add the dry ingredients to the wet ingredients a little at a time, mixing until just combined.
4. Fill the cupcake liners to halfway and bake for 17–20 minutes or until a skewer inserted into the center of the cupcake comes out clean. Leave to cool slightly for about 5 minutes before turning out onto a rack. These cakes do settle a bit after baking and seem moister within an hour or so after baking.
5. For the icing, cream the cream cheese in your mixer until soft. Mix in the port and beat well again. Gradually add the confectioner's sugar to taste.
6. Ice the cupcakes and dust with a little cake glitter.

ALTERNATIVES:
♥ Any sweet wine, fortified blend or sherry will work.

Tip: Don't over-mix your batter once dry ingredients are added. Just mix on low speed until incorporated. Always be gentle. As batters are overbeaten, they can thin out, causing fillings like fruit to sink and producing a poor crumb as well. If your batter does seem a bit thin, try sprinkling some of the filling such as berries on top just before baking.

Jägerbomb

This was one recipe that I really thought wouldn't work but I had to experiment as my friend Benita was coming to Cape Town for the holidays and this is one of her favorite party drinks. The end result was very surprising and I would definitely recommend that you try these for your next party!

3 cups cake flour

1½ cups sugar

4 t baking powder

1 t salt

½ cup milk

½ cup Red Bull

1 cup vegetable oil

4 large eggs

2 T vanilla extract

ICING

½ cup butter or margarine

2½ cups sifted confectioner's sugar

4 T Jägermeister

DECORATIONS

Multi-colored sugar crystals

Cake glitter dust

1. Preheat your oven to 350°F and line 24 cupcake molds or muffin tins with paper liners.
2. Sift all the dry ingredients together. Add the milk, Red Bull, oil, eggs and vanilla to the dry ingredients and beat well until smooth and creamy.
3. Fill the cupcake liners to halfway and bake for 17–20 minutes or until a skewer inserted into the center of the cupcake comes out clean. Leave to cool slightly for about 5 minutes before turning out onto a rack.
4. For the icing, cream the butter well in the electric mixer. Gradually add half of the confectioner's sugar until it is thoroughly combined. Alternate adding a little of the Jägermeister at a time with the rest of the confectioner's sugar until your icing looks thick enough to spread or pipe.
5. Ice the cupcakes, roll the sides in the sugar crystals and dust with a little cake glitter.

ALTERNATIVES:
♥ Add a little food coloring to the cake batter such as yellow and then a different color (such as green) to the icing to get that bomb effect.

Tip: When making icing with an electric mixer, use your paddle attachment as the whisk attachment will result in your icing being too fluffy with lots of air bubbles, which you don't want.

Southern red velvet

Every week at the Cape Cake & Candy Company, we make hundreds of our red velvet cupcakes—these are super moist and have that classic buttermilk and vinegar tartness. Sitting together one evening, my friend Tania and I were discussing red velvet cake and its Southern origins and decided to try it combined with another Southern classic. These were a hit!

The spices in the Southern Comfort add an extra depth to the subtle coffee and cocoa elements in the cupcakes and they are definitely worth trying!

2¼ cups cake flour
1 t baking soda)
1 t baking powder
2 T unsweetened cocoa powder
1 t salt
1¾ cups sugar
1 cup vegetable oil
2 large eggs
1 cup buttermilk
2 t vanilla extract
1 t red gel food coloring
½ cup strong hot coffee
1 t white distilled vinegar

GLAZE
2½ cups sifted confectioner's sugar
5 T Southern Comfort

ICING
1 cup full-fat cream-cheese
2 T Southern Comfort
½ cup sifted confectioner's sugar

DECORATIONS
Cake glitter dust

1. Preheat your oven to 350°F and line 24 cupcake molds or muffin tins with paper liners.
2. In a medium bowl, whisk together the flour, baking soda (baking soda), baking powder, cocoa powder and salt.
3. In the mixing bowl, combine the sugar and oil. Add in the eggs, buttermilk, vanilla, and red food coloring. Mix in the coffee and vinegar. (Don't skip this step!) Add the dry ingredients to the wet ingredients a little at a time, mixing until just combined. The cake batter will appear to start bubbling a little at this point but this is normal.
4. Fill the cupcake liners to halfway and bake for 17–20 minutes or until a skewer inserted into the center of the cupcake comes out clean. Leave to cool. Do not remove from the tins/molds.
5. To make the glaze, whisk together the ingredients. While the cupcakes are cooling in the tins/molds, poke several holes in the top of the cakes and soak the glaze mixture into the top with a pastry brush (you should have enough to do each cupcake twice).
6. For the icing, cream the cream cheese in your mixer until soft. Mix in the Southern Comfort and beat well again. Gradually add the confectioner's sugar to taste. Ice the cupcakes and dust with a little cake glitter.

ALTERNATIVES:
♥ Jack Daniel's / brandy

Tip: Instead of poking holes in the top of the cupcake and using a pastry brush to infuse the alcohol in, buy a syringe from the pharmacy and inject the alcohol into the cupcakes, making 3–4 holes. Don't inject any further than about a ⅓ of the way down as too deep will cause the bottom of the cupcake to become soggy.

Pimm's, orange & lemonade

When we lived in Bahrain, one of our favorite activities was to congregate at the communal pool, each bringing some drinks and snacks. Sasha's classic cocktail was a HUGE jug of Pimm's No. 1 with lemonade and fresh fruit. In the 113°F heat, it was one of our favorite refreshments! I'm dedicating this cupcake to all of the girls on Atlanta 3, who I'm sure will enjoy it just as much as the cocktail.

2 cups cake flour
1 t baking soda
1 t baking powder
1 t salt
2 cups sugar
1 cup vegetable oil
2 large eggs
½ cup buttermilk
2 T vanilla extract
1 t white distilled vinegar
1 cup Pimm's No. 1
Zest of 1 orange

FILLING
4 strawberries
10 raspberries
2 slices of peeled orange
2 slices of peeled cucumber

ICING
½ cup butter or margarine
2½ cups sifted confectioner's sugar
4 T Pimm's No. 1

DECORATIONS
Fresh fruit slices
Mint leaves
Cake glitter dust

1. Preheat your oven to 350°F and line 24 cupcake molds or muffin tins with paper liners.
2. In a medium bowl, sift together the flour, baking soda (baking soda), baking powder and salt.
3. In the mixing bowl, combine the sugar and oil. Add the rest of the wet ingredients. Add the dry ingredients to the wet ingredients a little at a time, mixing until just combined.
4. Fill the cupcake liners to halfway and bake for 17–20 minutes or until a skewer inserted into the center of the cupcake comes out clean. Leave to cool slightly for about 5 minutes before turning out onto a rack.
5. Using an apple-corer, small round cookie cutter or a small knife, cut holes in the top of the cooled cupcakes about 1½–2cm deep. Remove the excess cake and keep the tops as lids.
6. For the filling, blend the fruit to make a thick purée. Fill the cupcakes and pop the lids back on.
7. To make the icing, cream the butter well in the electric mixer. Gradually add half of the confectioner's sugar until it is well combined. Alternate adding a little of the Pimm's at a time with the rest of the confectioner's sugar until your icing looks thick enough to spread or pipe. Ice the cupcakes, top with some fresh fruit slices and mint leaves, and dust with a little cake glitter.

Note: Because of the fresh fruit in this cupcake, they should be kept refrigerated and eaten on the same day as assembled.

ALTERNATIVES:
♥ Any fresh fruit mix that you prefer—extra cucumber is especially refreshing!

Tip: Adding the confectioner's sugar a little at a time makes a big difference—your icing will be less grainy and much more light and fluffy.

Lemon-ginger martini

My friend Tania is a huge help whenever I get stuck for recipe ideas. She usually goes to the bottle store and looks for inspiration. Invariably, though, as she stands there intensely looking at all the liquor on the shelves, a shop assistant will come asking her if she needs help. She always answers: "No thanks, I'm just looking for inspiration!" The look of confusion on their faces is priceless. One moment of inspiration came recently when we found a bottle of iced-cake flavored vodka. It seemed very natural to put this new flavor in a cupcake but then I had to decide what to pair it with.

These cupcakes are very fresh and tangy and if you make a real lemon-ginger martini, the two go together beautifully!

3 cups cake flour

1½ cups sugar

4 t baking powder

1 t salt

½ cup milk

½ cup iced-cake flavored vodka

1 cup vegetable oil

4 large eggs

2 t lemon juice

Zest of 1 lemon

2 T finely grated ginger root

ICING

½ cup butter or margarine

2½ cups sifted confectioner's sugar

3 T iced-cake flavored vodka

1 T lemon juice

DECORATIONS

Finely chopped preserved stem ginger

Lemon zest

Cake glitter dust

1. Preheat your oven to 350°F and line 24 cupcake molds or muffin tins with paper liners.

2. Sift all the dry ingredients together straight into the mixing bowl. Add the milk, vodka, oil, eggs, lemon juice, lemon zest and grated ginger to the dry ingredients and beat well until smooth and creamy.

3. Fill the cupcake liners to just over halfway and bake for 17–20 minutes or until a skewer inserted into the center of the cupcake comes out clean. Leave to cool for about 5 minutes before turning out onto a rack.

4. To make the icing, cream the butter well in the electric mixer. Gradually add half of the confectioner's sugar until it is thoroughly combined. Alternate adding a little of the vodka and lemon juice at a time with the rest of the confectioner's sugar until your icing looks thick enough to spread or pipe.

5. Ice the cupcakes, sprinkle the chopped preserved stem ginger and lemon zest on top of the piped icing and dust with a little cake glitter.

ALTERNATIVES:

♥ You don't have to use iced-cake flavored vodka for this recipe. Try other flavors and adjust the lemon and ginger to other variations to suit the vodka—such as raspberry for example.

Tip: If you don't have a piping bag or parchment paper to make a piping bag, use a sandwich bag and fill it with as much icing as you're comfortable to pipe with. You can always refill it again if you run out. Cut off a small piece of the corner. This will result in a smooth piped look, not as frilly as the star nozzle, but just as pretty.

Super Cosmo

This book wouldn't have been complete without a classic Cosmo cupcake. The Cosmopolitan cocktail came back into fashion with the appearance of Carrie Bradshaw and her friends in *Sex in the City* and the cupcake version has appeared in a number of recipe books since then. I played around with these recipes but decided that they were either pretty but had no substance; were pretty awful; or were too complicated. Going back to basics, I deconstructed the cocktail, used my super-easy, all-in-one-bowl recipe and voila—the Super Cosmo was born!

3 cups cake flour
1½ cups sugar
4 t baking powder
1 t salt
½ cup milk
3 T vodka
2 T triple sec
2 T lime cordial
2 T cranberry juice
1 cup vegetable oil
4 large eggs
2 t vanilla extract
Pink food coloring (optional)

ICING
½ cup butter or margarine
2½ cups sifted confectioner's sugar
1 t vodka
1 t triple sec
1 t lime cordial
1 t cranberry juice
Pink food coloring (optional)

DECORATIONS
Fresh lime slice, quartered
Pink sugar crystals
Cake glitter dust

1. Preheat your oven to 350°F and line 24 cupcake molds or muffin tins with paper liners.
2. Sift all the dry ingredients together straight into the mixing bowl. Add the milk, vodka, triple sec, lime cordial, cranberry juice, oil, eggs and vanilla to the dry ingredients and beat well until smooth and creamy.
3. Fill the cupcake liners to halfway and bake for 17–20 minutes or until a skewer inserted into the center of the cupcake comes out clean. Leave to cool for about 5 minutes before turning out onto a rack.
4. For the icing, cream the butter well in the electric mixer. Gradually add half of the confectioner's sugar until it is thoroughly combined.
5. Combine the liquid ingredients in a cup and alternate adding a little of this mixture at a time with the rest of the confectioner's sugar until your icing looks thick enough to spread or pipe.
6. Ice the cupcakes, top with a fresh lime quarter on top of the piped icing and dust with a little pink sugar and cake glitter.

ALTERNATIVES:
♥ The cranberry juice will give your cupcakes a very pale pink color. If you want the classic Cosmo look, add a tiny drop of pink food coloring to the batter and icing.

Tip: Place your mixing bowl (if you have a stainless steel bowl) and mixing tool in the fridge for 5 minutes before making your icing—the cold bowl and arms will make stiffer peaks in your icing.

Caramel vodka

We were invited to a dinner at a friends' just recently where I first tasted caramel-flavored vodka. Our host suggested that I try this as a cupcake and a new favorite was created. I'm dedicating these cupcakes to Dawn who was the inspiration, as they're classy, stylish and sweet—just like her.

3 cups cake flour

1½ cups sugar

4 t baking powder

1 t salt

1 cup milk

1 cup vegetable oil

4 large eggs

2 t caramel essence

5 T caramel-flavored vodka

5 T caramel-flavored vodka (to saturate cupcakes)

ICING

½ cup butter or margarine

2½ cups sifted confectioner's sugar

2 T caramel-flavored vodka

½ tin Caramel Treat

DECORATIONS

Wilson's Crème Caramels (grated)

Gold cake glitter dust

1. Preheat your oven to 350°F and line 24 cupcake molds or muffin tins with paper liners.

2. Sift all the dry ingredients together. Add the milk, oil, eggs, caramel essence and vodka to the dry ingredients and beat well until smooth and creamy.

3. Fill each of the cupcake liners to just over halfway full. Bake for 17–20 minutes or until a skewer inserted into the cupcake comes out clean. Leave to cool. Do not remove from the tins/molds.

4. While the cupcakes are cooling in the tins/molds, poke several holes in the top of the cakes and use a pastry brush to saturate the tops of the cupcakes with the caramel vodka (about half a teaspoon per cupcake).

5. To make the icing, cream the butter well in the electric mixer. Gradually add half of the confectioner's sugar until it is thoroughly combined. Alternate adding a little of the vodka at a time with the rest of the confectioner's sugar until your icing looks thick enough to spread or pipe. Mix in the Treat.

6. Ice the cupcakes, sprinkle the grated Crème Caramels on top of the piped icing and dust with a little gold cake glitter.

ALTERNATIVES:
♥ For a non-alcoholic version, leave out the vodka. For the icing, use 1 t of caramel essence instead.
♥ Add a sprinkle of course salt on top for a salted-caramel flavor.

Tip: You can freeze buttercream icing for up to four months. I put leftover icing in a freezer bag and label it with the type and date. Once defrosted you simply have to squeeze it out of the bag and beat it again.

Milk tart & tequila

This recipe was created for my brother, Frans. Milk tart (a South African baked custard tart) is his all-time favorite and he can eat a whole pie all by himself!

When I found new tequila-based, milk-tart flavored liqueur, it was like a match made in heaven and the flavor, if you close your eyes, is exactly like the original version but with a definite kick!

3 cups cake flour

1½ cups sugar

4 t baking powder

1 t salt

1 cup milk

1 cup vegetable oil

4 large eggs

2 t vanilla extract

FILLING

½ cup cream—divide this into
   2 x ¼ cups

½ cup Kandi Milk Tart

2 T cornstarch

2 egg yolks

1 whole egg

5 T sugar

2 T butter

1 t vanilla extract

ICING

½ cup butter or margarine

2½ cups sifted confectioner's sugar

4 T Kandi™ Milk Tart

DECORATIONS

Ground cinnamon

Gold cake glitter dust

1. Preheat your oven to 350°F and line 24 cupcake molds or muffin tins with paper liners.

2. Sift all the dry ingredients together. Add the milk, oil, eggs and vanilla to the dry ingredients and beat well until smooth and creamy.

3. Fill the cupcake liners to halfway. Bake for 17-20 minutes for cupcakes or until a skewer inserted into the center of the cupcake comes out clean. Leave to cool for about 5 minutes before turning out onto a rack. Allow to cool completely.

4. For the filling, in a saucepan add ¼ cup of cream, Kandi Milk Tart and sugar. Bring this mixture to the boil and then remove from the stove.

5. In a medium bowl, whisk the cornstarch with the other ¼ cup of cream and then beat in the 2 egg yolks and 1 whole egg. Pour ⅓ of the boiling liqueur mix into the egg mix but remember to keep whisking as you add this so that the eggs don't cook. Pour the mixture from the bowl into the hot liqueur mix in the saucepan in a thin stream whisking all the time again.

6. Place the saucepan back on the heat and whisk constantly until the mixture reaches the consistency of very thick custard, remove from the heat and beat in the butter and the vanilla extract. Leave to one side to cool.

7. Using an apple-corer, small round cookie cutter or a knife, cut holes in the top of the cooled cupcakes about 1½-2cm deep. Remove the excess cake from the divots and keep the tops as lids. Spoon the filling into the holes and pop the little lids back on.

8. To make the icing, cream the butter well in the electric mixer. Gradually add half of the confectioner's sugar until it is thoroughly combined. Alternate adding a little of the Kandi Milk Tart at a time with the rest of the confectioner's sugar until your icing looks thick enough to spread or pipe.

9. Ice the cupcakes and dust with a little ground cinnamon and gold cake glitter.

ALTERNATIVES:

♥ This recipe works well with any cream liqueur; just leave out the cinnamon dusting.

Tip: Eggs separate best when cold, but whites whip best when at room temperature or warm.

Corona & lime

There has always been some dispute as to whether Corona (my favorite beer) is actually a beer or not. It says *cerveza* on the label, which is Spanish for beer so I'm sticking with my opinion that it is! I've focused mainly on wine and spirits, so this cupcake is dedicated to all the beer drinkers out there. I have had some requests to try this recipe with lager but I'll leave that to any kitchen chemists who may be feeling adventurous!

These cupcakes are soft and moist, and the lime has a fresh, acidic flavor which means that they are definitely moreish!

3 cups cake flour
1½ cups sugar
4 T baking powder
1 t salt
1 cup Corona
1 cup vegetable oil
4 large eggs
1 T vanilla extract
Juice of 1 lime
Zest of 2 limes

ICING
1 cup full-fat cream-cheese
½ cup sifted confectioner's sugar
Juice of 1 lime

DECORATIONS
Mother of pearl cake glitter dust
Slices of lime, quartered

1. Preheat your oven to 350°F and line 24 cupcake molds or muffin tins with paper liners.
2. Sift all the dry ingredients together into a mixing bowl. Add the Corona, oil, eggs, vanilla and lime juice to the dry ingredients and beat well until smooth and creamy.
3. Fold in the lime zest and fill the cupcake liners to halfway. Bake for 17–20 minutes or until a skewer inserted into the center of the cupcake comes out clean. Leave to cool for about 5 minutes before turning out onto a rack.
4. For the icing, cream the cream cheese until soft. Mix in the lime juice and beat well again. Gradually add the confectioner's sugar to taste.
5. Ice the cupcakes, dust with a little cake glitter and top with a quartered slice of lime.

ALTERNATIVES:
♥ Substitute Blue Moon beer for the Corona and add orange juice and zest instead of the lime.

Tip: Chill your icing in the fridge for a little while before you pipe—this makes it firmer and it holds its shape better.

Painkiller

The Painkiller is the official drink of the British Virgin Islands and was originally trademarked by Pusser's Rum. Legend has it that the drink originated at the Soggy Dollar Bar at White Bay on the island of Jost Van Dyke. This bar has its own great story but in a nutshell, it's one of the few bars in the BVI without a dingy dock and you have to swim ashore—hence paying for your drinks with soggy dollars!

While the official recipe for the Painkiller is a secret, and every bar in the islands has its own version, we actually don't really care. We know it contains pineapple juice, orange juice, Coco Lopez cream of coconut, rum, is topped with freshly grated nutmeg and is delicious, which is all that really matters!

The Coco Lopez cream of coconut is difficult to come by here in South Africa so I've made some adjustments using coconut cream, which I hope does the cocktail justice.

3 cups cake flour

1½ cups sugar

4 t baking powder

1 t salt

1 t powdered nutmeg

¼ cup rum

¼ cup coconut cream

¼ cup fresh orange juice

¼ cup pineapple juice

1 cup vegetable oil

4 large eggs

2 t vanilla extract

ICING

6 T coconut cream

2½ cups sifted confectioner's sugar

2 T dark rum

DECORATIONS

Grated nutmeg

Pineapple flowers

Cake glitter dust

1. Preheat your oven to 350°F and line 24 cupcake molds or muffin tins with paper liners.

2. Sift all the dry ingredients together straight into the mixing bowl. Add the rum, coconut cream, pineapple juice, orange juice, oil, eggs and vanilla to the dry ingredients and beat well until smooth and creamy.

3. Fill the cupcake liners to halfway and bake for 17–20 minutes or until a skewer inserted into the center of the cupcake comes out clean. Leave to cool for about 5 minutes before turning out onto a rack.

4. To make the icing, cream the coconut well in the electric mixer. Gradually add half of the confectioner's sugar until it is thoroughly combined. Alternate adding a little of the rum at a time with the rest of the confectioner's sugar until your icing looks thick enough to spread or pipe.

5. To make pineapple flowers, peel 1 whole pineapple making sure that the eyes have all been removed. Slice the pineapple as thinly as possible without the slices falling apart and place on a baking tray. Bake at 250°F for 30 minutes then turn over and bake for another hour or until the slices have completely dried out but are still flexible. Place the slices in

cupcake liners and leave in the warm oven (that has been turned OFF) to set overnight. These can be stored in an airtight container for up to 2 weeks.

6. Ice the cupcakes, sprinkle with nutmeg and top with a pineapple flower just before serving. Dust with a little cake glitter.

Note: Do not store the decorated cupcakes as the moisture from the icing will cause the pineapple flowers to wilt.

ALTERNATIVES:

♥ If you're in a rush, top the cupcakes with some store-bought dried pineapple.

Tip: Always wait for cupcakes to cool completely before frosting. Even the slightest warmth from a cupcake can quickly turn your frosting or icing into a mess.

Lemon-limoncello

My all-time favorite dessert is lemon meringue tart so this recipe was just for me, just because. It is heavenly!

3 cups cake flour

1½ cups sugar

4 t baking powder

1 t salt

¾ cup milk

¼ cup lemon juice

1 cup vegetable oil

4 large eggs

2 T vanilla extract

Zest of 1 lemon

FILLING

½ cup cream—divide this into 2
   x ¼ cups

½ cup limoncello

5 T sugar

2 T cornstarch

2 egg yolks

1 whole egg

2 T butter

1 t vanilla extract

TOPPING

2 egg whites

1 cup sifted confectioner's sugar

DECORATIONS

Cake glitter dust

1. Preheat your oven to 350°F and line 24 cupcake molds or muffin tins with paper liners.
2. Sift all the dry ingredients together into a mixing bowl. Add the milk, lemon juice, oil, eggs and vanilla to the dry ingredients and beat well until smooth and creamy. Fold in the lemon zest and fill the cupcake liners to halfway.
3. Bake for 17–20 minutes or until a skewer inserted into the center of the cupcake comes out clean. Leave to cool for about 5 minutes before turning out onto a rack.
4. To make the filling, in a saucepan add ¼ cup of cream, limoncello and sugar and bring this mixture to the boil and then remove from the stove.
5. In a medium bowl, whisk the cornstarch with the other ¼ cup of cream and then beat in the 2 egg yolks and 1 whole egg. Pour ⅓ of the boiling limoncello mix into the egg mix but remember to keep whisking as you add so that the eggs don't cook.
6. Pour the mixture from the bowl into the hot liqueur mix in the saucepan in a thin stream whisking all the time again. Place the saucepan back on the heat and whisk constantly until the mixture reaches the consistency of very thick custard, remove from the heat and beat in the butter and the vanilla extract. Leave to one side to cool.
7. Using an apple-corer, small round cookie cutter or a knife, cut holes in the top of the cooled cupcakes about 1½–2cm deep. Remove the excess cake from the divots and keep the tops

as lids. Spoon the cooled filling into the holes in the cupcakes and pop the little lids back on.

8. For the topping, whisk the egg whites on a medium-high speed until they are thick and glossy and form soft peaks in the bowl. Add the confectioner's sugar a little at a time until all is combined. Pipe the meringue onto the tops of the cakes immediately and place under a very low grill.

Note: Serve the cupcakes on the same day as they are made or, at best, the following day as stored meringue will start to break down.

ALTERNATIVES:
♥ If you're in a rush, store-bought lemon curd will do for the filling but add confectioner's sugar to thicken if you're adding the limoncello to the curd.

Tip: When mixing egg whites for meringue, use a paper towel to wipe all utensils and the bowl (including the mixer whisk attachment) with vinegar or lemon juice before they come in contact with the egg whites. Any trace of grease, will stop your egg whites from whipping up.

Strawberry daiquiri

These super-easy cupcakes are always a hit—especially at girly parties like bridal showers. They are the girl's equivalent of the Captain Morgan & Coke cupcakes. In this recipe I've substituted the oil for apple sauce which cuts the calories dramatically, making them practically guilt-free!

3 cups cake flour

1½ cups sugar

4 t baking powder

1 t salt

¼ cup light rum

¼ cup strawberry liqueur

½ cup milk

1 cup apple sauce

4 large eggs

1 t strawberry essence

Pink food coloring (optional)

ICING

½ cup butter or margarine

2½ cups sifted confectioner's sugar

4 T light rum

Pink food coloring (optional)

DECORATIONS

Mint leaves, sliced fresh strawberries or lime zest

Cake glitter dust

1. Preheat your oven to 350°F and line 24 cupcake molds or muffin tins with paper liners. Sift all the dry ingredients together straight into the mixing bowl. Add the rum, strawberry liqueur, milk, apple sauce, eggs, essence and coloring (optional) to the dry ingredients and beat well until smooth and creamy.

2. Fill the cupcake liners to halfway and bake for 17–20 minutes or until a skewer inserted into the center of the cupcake comes out clean. Leave to cool slightly for about 5 minutes before turning out onto a rack.

3. To make the icing, cream the butter well. Gradually add half of the confectioner's sugar until it is thoroughly combined. Alternate adding a little of the light rum at a time with the rest of the confectioner's sugar until your icing looks thick enough to spread or pipe.

4. Ice the cupcakes, sprinkle with lime zest, or top with fresh mint leaves or sliced fresh strawberries, and dust with a little cake glitter.

ALTERNATIVES:

♥ To make a virgin daiquiri, use milk instead of vodka in the batter and lime juice instead of rum in the icing.

Tip: When placing fruit that has been soaking in syrup or juice on top of icing, always make sure the fruit is completely dry. If not, the juice may run into the icing causing ugly stains or resulting in the icing splitting around the juice making it look curdled. Dry the fruit well on a paper towel and allow to air dry for about half an hour before decorating.

Shirley Temple

I simply *had* to put one non-alcoholic cupcake in this book: this cocktail has very special memories for as me, it was what we always ordered for my sister when we went out for dinner as a family. Although Tammy is now all grown up, is a qualified chiropractor running a clinic in Kuala Lumpur, she is ten years younger than me and will always be my baby sister.

3 cups + 2 T cake flour
1½ cups sugar
4 t baking powder
1 t salt
1 cup Sprite/lemonade
1 cup vegetable oil
4 large eggs
2 t vanilla extract
1 T maraschino cherry juice
Red food coloring

ICING

½ cup butter or margarine
2½ cups sifted confectioner's sugar
2 T lemon juice
1 T maraschino cherry juice

DECORATIONS

24 maraschino/glazed cherries
Cake glitter dust

1. Preheat your oven to 350°F and line 24 cupcake molds or muffin tins with paper liners.
2. Sift all the dry ingredients (excluding the 2 T of flour) together in a mixing bowl. Add the lemonade, oil, eggs and vanilla to the dry ingredients and beat well until smooth and creamy.
3. Spoon 1 cup of the batter into a separate bowl and mix in the 2 T of flour, the maraschino juice and the food coloring. Spoon this mixture into the bottom of the cupcake liners. Fill the cupcake liners to halfway with the remaining batter, being careful not to mix the two layers.
4. Bake for 17–20 minutes or until a skewer inserted into the center of the cupcake comes out clean. Leave to cool for about 5 minutes before turning out onto a rack.
5. To make the icing, cream the butter well in the electric mixer. Gradually add half of the confectioner's sugar until it is thoroughly combined. Alternate adding a little of the cherry and lemon juice at a time with the rest of the confectioner's sugar until your icing looks thick enough to spread or pipe. Top with a maraschino cherry with a stalk and dust with a little cake glitter.

ALTERNATIVES:
♥ For an extra fruity surprise, pop a maraschino/glazed cherry into the cupcake batter before baking. This will sink to the bottom but is a lovely surprise when you bite into it.

Tip: When decorating, ice a few cupcakes at a time and finish these with all the decorations. Doing a large batch all at once, especially on very warm days, means that the icing on the first cakes may have formed a slightly dry crust or skin already and sprinkles and glitter may not stick as well as if it was freshly iced.

Bloody Mary

Everybody has his or her own hangover cure—whether it's plain old aspirin and a large glass of water or downing a Hair of the Dog. The most common morning-after drink is the Bloody Mary. This book wouldn't have been complete without a final cure for having sampled all the cakes that have gone before!

This cupcake was really fun to put together—I was worried about the combination of sweet and hot but it works VERY well—the taste is unusual but super yummy! It's spicy and delicious and definitely falls into the adult category—not only because of the vodka, but also because the icing has some serious kick!

This final recipe is dedicated to *all* of my friends. I dare you to try it—just so we can start all over again!

3 cups cake flour

1½ cups sugar

4 t baking powder

1 t celery salt

½ t black pepper

¼ t cayenne pepper

½ cup tomato juice

¼ cup vodka

1 T lemon juice

2 t Tabasco sauce

2 t Worcestershire sauce

1 T horseradish sauce

1 cup vegetable oil

4 large eggs

ICING

½ cup butter or margarine

2½ cups sifted confectioner's sugar

1 t celery salt

1 T vodka

1 t lemon juice

1 t cayenne pepper

DECORATIONS

Cake glitter dust

Celery (optional)

1. Preheat your oven to 350°F and line 24 cupcake molds or muffin tins with paper liners.

1. Sift all the dry ingredients together straight into the mixing bowl. Add the tomato juice, vodka, lemon juice, hot sauce, Worcestershire sauce, horseradish sauce, oil, and eggs to the dry ingredients and beat well until smooth and creamy.

2. Fill each of the cupcake liners to just over halfway. Be careful not to overfill. Bake for 17–20 minutes or until a skewer inserted into the center of the cupcake comes out clean. Leave to cool for about 5 minutes before turning out onto a rack.

3. To make the icing, cream the butter well in an electric mixer. Gradually add half of the confectioner's sugar until it is thoroughly combined. Alternate adding the rest of the ingredients with the rest of the confectioner's sugar until your mixture looks thick enough to spread or pipe. Ice your cupcakes, dust with a little gold cake glitter and top off with a small celery stalk.

ALTERNATIVES:

♥ For a non-alcoholic version, replace the vodka with an equal amount of tomato juice in the batter. In the icing, use milk instead of the vodka.

Tip: If you're feeling very creative, you can make small celery stalks out of fondant to decorate your cupcakes.

Acknowledgments

Thank you to my family and friends, without whom this book wouldn't have happened. Thank you especially to my husband, Ken. I dedicate this entire book to you. I can't express enough how much your support, encouragement and testing helped!

First published in 2014
Copyright © Metz Press 2014
Text copyright © Simone Balman
Photographs copyright © Metz Press

First Skyhorse Publishing Edition 2018

Visit our website at www.skyhorsepublishing.com.

10 9 8 7 6 5 4 3 2 1

Library of Congress Cataloging-in-Publication Data is available on file.

Print ISBN: 978-1-5107-3016-8
E-Book ISBN: 978-1-5107-3021-2

Printed in China

PUBLISHER
Wilsia Metz

EDITOR
Nikki Metz

PHOTOGRAPHER
Ivan Naude

DESIGNER
Liezl Maree

DTP
Richards DTP Studios

PROOFREADER
Carla Masson

REPRODUCTION
Color/Fuzion, Green Point